Meditation

Complete Guide to Relieving Stress and Living a Peaceful Life

TABLE OF CONTENTS

INTRODUCTION

I can tell you are a brilliant person because you made the choice to purchase this book. I believe that you will learn a great deal of information and that you will open your eyes and gain a new perspective in your life.

With life being so hectic in this day and age, it is no wonder that people are seeking a way to find relaxation. Stress is a state of mind that many are suffering from as a result of their unhealthy lifestyles and the fast pace in which we live. The problems associated with stress go further than simply a mental imbalance and a feeling of edginess. Stress can result in a long term mental condition and can manifest itself physically in the form of many different physical disorders. The primary disorders that manifest are anxiety disorders and heart conditions. Stressors can have seriously negative effects on other aspects of your physical health as well, such as blood pressure and overall mental stability. You need to be aware that stress can lead to serious illness including cardiovascular diseases and the potential onset of cancer. Thus, this has a serious impact on lives today, tomorrow and in the near future. Instead of letting stress take over, people are becoming aware of the need for a certain amount of relaxation and are seeking it in many different ways.

Living a life that is hectic without any relief can cause you to develop depression, insomnia and other psychological problems. While it may start as a small issue, it can slowly develop into a larger, unbearable issue. You will find that your body becomes weaker, along with your immune system and self-esteem. Your body will be less likely to fight off common bacteria, like the common cold, headaches and similar ailments. This is why psychologists believe that stress is the root of many different disorders. It is important to realize and keep in mind that while much of life is outside of our control, what we can control is ourselves, our actions and our destiny.

1

MEDITATION

There are many alternatives open to people that wish to take charge of their lives which is vital. Stress can lead to blood pressure problems, which can lead to more serious health hazards, and it's time to re-appraise your lifestyle to see if your stress levels are acceptable or whether you can benefit from meditation. There are many who dismiss meditation as being something that is difficult to do, or something silly. However, it is easier than you might imagine.

Although you do have a choice of different methods of relaxation that are available in today's world such as yoga, acupuncture, massage and a change to your lifestyle; meditation is something that you can include in your current lifestyle to make it a more viable way to live. This book is written for the uninitiated in an effort to introduce them to different forms of meditation, so that individual readers can chose which method which fits best with their character and their lifestyle.

Meditation is a form of relaxation that has been practiced for thousands of years. It is mainly used for the treatment of anxiety but can be used for spiritual purposes as well. In this book, you will have the opportunity to read about the various ways in which meditation can be beneficial to your health. We introduce the overall concept of meditation in Chapter 2 and then we will break it down in subsequent chapters. You will be surprised at how many different kinds of meditation there are, and one of the available options will inevitably be suitable for you.

We also look at the different types of meditations from a practical point of view so that you can see which type of meditation can help you to achieve peace of mind and the ability to relax. You may believe that meditation is for the tree-hugging brigade, but you couldn't be further from the truth. It's a system that helps people to become grounded, happy and sometimes even more effective in the high profile jobs that they have. It isn't a craze or something that is only done by people who have too much time on their hands. It helps everyone equally who is willing to try it. While it helps to treat various diseases, it also helps to prevent the same diseases from developing.

MEDITATION

The main aim of the book will be to give you a guide to meditation and help you to understand the principles and practice of meditation. You may learn about techniques you have never heard of before, but these may be suitable to incorporate into your life to make your life a much more satisfying place to be.

A Great Alternative to Medication Therapy

Many people have found that meditation can greatly reduce the amount of medication they take on a daily basis, and over time, it can completely replace the medication that you take. In studies, meditation has shown significant strides in its ability to treat medical conditions that were previously treated by medication. Many doctors have found themselves recommending meditation before they recommend medication, which shows how powerful this simple action can be.

The importance of meditation is especially true for people who have heart disease, heart problems, blood pressure problems, anxiety, depression, and many other mental disorders.

What is Relaxation?

In common terminology, relaxation means that we leave ourselves free of tension. Relaxing mind may mean that the mind is not under stress or active. In today's lifestyle, this looks difficult. Doesn't it?
Now a day, most of us believe to be being under stress during most of the week and relax only on the weekends. This is considered the common way of life. Is this the right way of living? Is living a relaxed life all the time not our right? Let us reclaim it.

Bad stress:

If you ask anyone why they're under stress most of the week, what answer do you expect to get? 'I have so much work to do, deadlines to meet, tasks to be completed, prepare for the new launch', etc. Don't you think that something like this is the response?

Let us discuss why most of us are stressed all the time. At some time in our life, while we are chasing dreams we lose our habit of sitting back and reflecting. We begin giving auto responses. If we are held up in a traffic jam, our response is either to worry about the work ahead, blame the system, or some as such negative thought. Not many of us think 'Alright. If the traffic isn't moving, let's relax and listen to some good music, go back to some childhood memories, remember good friends, let me make the best use of the time to relax and enjoy life'. Not many of us respond in this way. We respond in stressed ways whenever we come across any similar situation. This habit is taking a big toll on our quality of life.

What is Meditation?

Meditation is both an art and a science. Meditation is in fact the training of the brain so that it is able to retain positive thought and banish negative thought

The act of meditation is not a single entity. It is a group of training exercises that focus on the mind. Meditation can improve mental health and physical health. Many of the techniques involved in meditation are easy to learn, and you can learn them from a book, article, or guidance from a meditation specialist.

Most of the techniques that you use in meditation involve the following components:

> ➢ Sitting or lying in a relaxed position.

> ➢ Deep breathing – you breathe deeply enough to get enough oxygen to relax your muscles. You should exhale deeply enough to completely empty your lungs.

MEDITATION

- ➤ Stop thinking of everyday problems and matters in your life. Clear your mind completely.

- ➤ Concentrate on your thoughts on a sound, a repeated word, an image, a concept or a feeling. You should point all of your attention to this one specific topic.

- ➤ When foreign thoughts make their way into your thought process, exhale and go back to your object of meditation. The purpose is to learn not to break your focus on your concentration point.

There are different meditation techniques to use, according to the degree of concentration and how you personally handle foreign thoughts. In many cases, the objective is to concentrate so hard on a specific thing that no foreign thoughts occur. When foreign thoughts enter your mind, you are to force them out and bring your concentration back. After enough practice, you will be able to prevent foreign thoughts from entering your mind.

Other techniques are completed in a manner that foreign thoughts have the capability of popping up. When these foreign thoughts do develop, the person is to stop and go back to pure meditation, in a relaxed manner. Thoughts that come up are typically things you have forgotten, suppressed or find material in nature. Many times, meditation allows you to rediscover material that you have hidden from yourself. The act of rediscovery will have psychotherapeutic effects.

If you have had a traumatic experience, meditation can help you to get past the event by allowing you to control the thoughts and re-design the traumatic event in your mind. The purpose of this is to take back control of your past so that your present can become more positive in nature. It can change your life for the better, as long as you are able to manipulate your though process in a positive manner.

The Effects of Meditation

Meditation has the following effects:

1. Meditation will give you rest and recreation.

2. You learn to relax.

3. You learn to concentrate better on problem solving.

4. Meditation often has a good effect upon the blood pressure.

5. Meditation has beneficial effects upon inner body processes, like circulation, respiration and digestion.

6. Regular meditation will have a psychotherapeutically effect.

7. Regular meditation will facilitate the immune system.

8. Meditation is usually pleasant.

The Difference between Hypnosis and Meditation

Hypnosis may have some of the same relaxing and psychotherapeutic effects as meditation. However, when you meditate you are in control yourself; by hypnosis you let some other person or some mechanical device control you. Also hypnosis will not have a training effect upon the ability to concentrate.

Hypnosis allows someone else to control your subconscious. This means that you are not in control of the events that are going on in your head during hypnosis. This can be extremely dangerous, especially if the person who is hypnotizing you is not experienced enough to properly enter the subconscious or follow the ethical guidelines that are set forth by hypnosis.

If you are trying to become calm and live a serene life, allowing someone else to manipulate your subconscious is not a positive way to do this. You want to be in control of your subconscious at all times and meditation allows you to do this.

A Simple Form of Meditation

Here is a simple form of meditation:

1. Sit in a good chair in a comfortable position.

2. Relax all your muscles as well as you can.

3. Stop thinking about anything, or at least try not to think about anything.

4. Breath out, relaxing all the muscles in your breathing apparatus.

5. Repeat the following in 10 – 20 minutes:

— Breath in so deep that you feel you get enough oxygen.

— Breath out, relaxing your chest and diaphragm completely.

— Every time you breathe out, think the word "one" or another simple word inside yourself. You should think the word in a prolonged manner, and so that you hear it inside you, but you should try to avoid using your mouth or voice.

6. If foreign thoughts come in, just stop these thoughts in a relaxed manner, and keep on concentrating upon the breathing and the word you repeat.

As you proceed through this meditation, you should feel steadily more relaxed in your mind and body. You will feel that you breathe steadily more effectively, and that the blood circulation throughout your body gets more efficient. You may also feel an increasing mental pleasure throughout the meditation. You will feel fully relaxed and at peace with your current situation, no matter what it is.

MEDITATION

The Effects of Meditation on Diseases

As any kind of training, meditation may be exaggerated so that you get tired and worn out. Therefore you should not meditate so long or so concentrated that you feel tired or mentally emptied.

Meditation may sometimes cause problems for people suffering from mental diseases, epilepsy, serious heart problems or neurological diseases. On the other hand, meditation may be of help in the treatment of these conditions and other conditions that are not mentioned here.

People suffering from such conditions should check out what effects the different kinds of meditation have on their own kind of health problems, before beginning to practice meditation, and be cautious if they choose to begin to meditate. It may be wise to learn meditation from an experienced teacher, psychologist or health worker that use meditation as a treatment module for the actual disease.

You may also want to check with your primary care doctor to ensure that it is safe for you to meditate. This is especially true if you have any existing health problems that affect your breathing, your mental state, or your ability to stay awake.

Some disorders, especially ones that cause fatigue, can be made worse by meditation. Your doctor will be able to tell you whether it is safe for you to meditate on a regular basis, or how long you should meditate to avoid exhaustion.

Meditation as a Spiritual Exercise

According to Buddhism, a person can reach "Nirvana", or the highest state of enlightenment, through continuous meditation and by participating in the Buddha's daily service among other things. Through time, many people have benefited from the practice of meditation.

MEDITATION

Meditation, as practiced by Buddhist monks and practitioners, has become a spiritual tool and health enhancer in one. It's more than just the chants and meditative posture. Meditation is about proper breathing and concentration of one's thoughts. As a health and spiritual practice, meditation came into prominence centuries ago in the East where people's lives and culture demanded a way to "escape" the realities of life.

How do we know if we're already in a state of meditation or just wasting away with our eyes closed? Meditation is a state of mind that leads to inner peace, self-fulfillment, self- improvement, and the development of a positive outlook in life. There are two types of meditation; the concentrative and the mindfulness type. Concentrative is more on the person's concentration that is sitting quietly and calmly with good breathing patterns. It is said that the one's mind is somewhat connected to one's breath of air. Continuous rhythm of inhales and exhales of the breath will make the person feel calmer and relaxed, focusing on their steady flow of air in and out of their bodies. This will result in the mind being more aware and tranquil at the same time. Mindfulness, on the other hand, involves attention and awareness on passing waves of sensations, images, feelings, thoughts, sounds, and smell. Pretty much anything that your body can interact with. This, in turn, will give the person a more non-reactive mind state. Much like looking at a television without any feeling or thoughts that can bother you away.

Meditation and relaxation often go hand in hand. In scientific studies, it has been proven that there are health benefits in practicing this kind of activity. By being in a relaxed state of mind, the person is also regarded to as in alpha state, of which a level of consciousness that promotes good healing. Relaxation in a person is highly recommended since people always move and think and by being relaxed it can also give relaxation to the body and mind that will eventually enhance our well being.

Knowing all of this, one can see the connection of both scientific and religious factors all because of meditation. Indeed, this activity shows a unique philosophy that can really help oneself. In practicing such kind of relaxation process, the person sees the innermost self at its fullest. This helps the person in dealing with external difficulties, seeing past all this and in a way becomes humble and calm in dealing with situations. This relaxed state of meditating allows the person in helping oneself health-wise, since this to can take away simple headaches, stress, or even mild anxiety. It began way before, and it will never go away. This kind of activity brings out the person in you. By meditating, this will give you a sense of calmness in a positive state. There are no known facts that this can be harmful to you, so why don't you give it a try?

CHAPTER 1

What Is Meditation? And Other Questions Answered

"Feelings come and go like clouds in a windy sky. Conscious breathing is my anchor."

Thích Nhất Hạnh

Meditation 101

Meditation refers to a state in which your body and mind are consciously relaxed and focused. Practitioners of this art have reported increased awareness, focus, concentration, as well as a more positive outlook on life.

Meditation is most commonly associated with monks, mystics and other spiritual disciplines. However, you don't have to be a monk or a mystic to enjoy its benefits, and you certainly don't have to be in a special place to practice it. You could even try it in your own living room!

Though there are many different approaches to meditation, the fundamental principles remain the same. The most important among these principles is that of removing obstructive, negative, and wandering thoughts or fantasies, so you can calm the mind with a deep sense of focus. This clears the mind of debris and prepares it for a higher quality of activity.

The negative thoughts you have of those noisy neighbors, bossy officemates, that parking ticket you got, and unwanted spam are said to contribute to the 'polluting' of the mind. Shutting them out allows for the 'cleansing' of the mind so that it may focus on deeper, more meaningful thoughts.

Some practitioners even shut out all sensory input. That means there are no sights, no sounds, and nothing to touch so that they can try to detach themselves from the commotion around them. You may now focus on a deep, profound thought if this is your goal. It may seem deafening at first, since we are all too accustomed to constantly hearing and seeing things. But as you continue this exercise, you will find yourself becoming more aware of everything around you.

If you find the meditating positions you see on television threatening; the ones with impossibly arched backs and painful-looking contortions, you don't have to worry! The principle here is to be in a comfortable position conducive to concentration. This may be while sitting cross-legged, standing, lying down, and even walking.

If the position allows you to relax and focus, that would be a good starting point. While sitting or standing, the back should be straight, but not too tense or tight. In other positions, the only no-no is slouching and falling asleep.

Loose and comfortable clothes help a lot in the process of meditation since tight fitting clothes have a tendency to squeeze you and make you feel tense.

The place you perform meditation should have a soothing atmosphere. It may be in your living room, bedroom, or any place that you feel comfortable in. You might want to purchase an exercise mat if you plan to take on the more challenging positions (if you feel more focused doing so, and if the contortionist in you is screaming for release). You may want to have the place arranged so that it is soothing to your senses.

MEDITATION

Silence helps most people relax and meditate, so you may want a quiet and isolated area far from the ringing of the phone or the humming of the washing machine. Pleasing scents also help in that regard, so stocking up on aromatic candles isn't such a bad idea either.

The monks you see on television making those monotonous sounds are actually performing their mantra. This, in simple terms, is a short creed. A simple sound which these practitioners hold a mystic value. You do not need to perform such creeds; however, it would pay off to note that focusing on repeated actions such as breathing, and humming help the practitioner enter a higher state of consciousness.

The principle here is focus. You could try focusing on a certain object or thought, even while keeping your eyes open, focus on a single sight. One sample routine would be to, while in a meditative state, silently name every part of your body and focusing your consciousness on that part. While doing this you should be aware of any tension on any part of your body. Mentally visualize releasing this tension. It does in fact work wonders. There are also many meditation CDs on the market that have been scientifically proven to alter your brainwaves in such a way to help you achieve deep meditation. Find out more about these here: Meditation CDs.

In all, meditation is a relatively risk-free practice and its benefits are well worth the effort (or non-effort remembers we're relaxing).

Studies have shown that meditation does bring about beneficial physiologic effects to the body. There has been a growing consensus in the medical community to further study the effects of such meditation. Start now in creating your health and well being... Meditate today!

Q: What is meditation?

A: Meditation is both an art and a science. Meditation is in fact the training of the brain so that it is able to retain positive thought and banish negative thought. It is referred to as a science because it

13

involves altering brain patterns, and the reason that it is also thought of as an art is because it requires a great deal of synchronization between the mind, body and soul (or subconscious mind). Through simple breathing techniques and concentration of different kinds, depending upon the meditation technique employed, the practitioner is able to help the mind and body to heal, to achieve spiritual thought and to embrace positivity and humility. These are all consciously part of the meditation process.

With practice, one can use meditation to relax and to recoil from the busy world. While individuals will have their own thoughts and feelings, meditation sets these aside and gives the individual something separate to focus upon. The concentration on breathing or upon other stimuli is what makes meditation so effective. The overall effect of meditation is that it helps the individual to feel a sense of well being that they would not have felt without the process of meditation. That's why meditation is so relevant to today's society.

Q: What are the origins and roots of meditation?

A: The origins of meditation can be traced back to ancient India. Monks in India are said to have practiced meditation extensively in order to develop a spiritual connection with god. It then slowly moved to the western world, where more and more people started to recognize the benefits that could be gained from meditation. This was also practiced by Buddhist monks in order to get closer to the moment in which they find themselves, so as to maximize the benefit of living a lifetime of humility and closer understanding of the nature of life. Monks today still practice meditation and it was meditation itself that brought about the philosophy behind Buddhist belief.

Indian scriptures, which are known as "Tantras," bear witness to the fact that meditation has been used for more than 5000 years. With this long history of success, there is little wonder why people are digging deeper into finding out what meditation is all about. Communes and retreats worldwide offer people an insight into meditation, though it is something that people can do on their own or even within a yoga class.

Today, thousands of people worldwide practice meditation to help them to beat stress and lead a much calmer life. Whether practiced in an Ashram or in a silent moment within your home, the roots of this great form of relaxation stand in testament of its effectiveness and ability to help people get closer to nature and more in touch with their beliefs. It is also thought that meditation helps the mind to be more controlled as mind and body come into harmony with each other through the process of meditation.

Q: What is the main purpose of meditation?

A: It has several benefits but the main purpose of meditation is to help people overcome stress and anxiety. Since stress can be associated with anguish that can cause illness, thus anything that diminishes that stress must be thought of as positive. This is the purpose of meditation. If you have a life that causes you mental concern and worry, then meditation can help you to be more focused. However, it should also be noted that many people use meditation in order to get closer to the truth within their lives. Buddhist meditation does just this, stripping life down to bare necessities and learning to breathe in a certain way that allows full acceptance of self.

Meditation helps in reducing stress and anxiety and slowly allows people to gain control over their minds and start making rational decisions. In fact, it's so good at helping give the practitioner clarity that many business people use meditation to help sharpen the skills of their workforce. The big push these days is for people to become more mindful and mindful meditation, as opposed to traditional meditation, helps people to focus on the things that are really important and let go of all things negative which may be holding them back or indeed causing them stress.

MEDITATION

Q: Who can perform it?

A: Meditation is mainly designed for people who are undergoing a lot of stress in their lives but it is also used for people to get closer to their roots or to their God. It is for those people who are finding it tough to cope with the everyday stresses and tensions and are constantly finding themselves having health problems because of those struggles. These health problems can be mental and physical in nature. That means that they may impair productivity. It might also be affecting a person's thinking capacity and reducing the amount of joy that a person can experience in their lives.

Meditation is great for people who want to become more positive. It's also suitable for those who have never tried it, since it has so many possibilities. If you don't feel that you suffer from stress, but know yourself to be busy, it may benefit you since it helps people to sleep well and also to remain centered. This balance in turn gives the body a chance to heal itself during the process of sleep. If you are someone who does not get sufficient sleep, you may find that meditation will help and although you don't see the lack of sleep as a problem, you should be aware that sleep is the process whereby the body has a chance to heal naturally. Thus, without it, you cannot live up to your own potential.

Q: How does stress come about?

A: There can be several triggers for stress. Daily work tensions, family problems, social pressures, psychological problems etc. are all triggers for stress. Many people forget to breathe correctly and that can cause them to develop tensions that can be alleviated by correct breathing techniques practiced in meditation. That may sound a little odd, but people are so busy with their lives that they need correct breathing techniques reinforced. If you have ever seen someone in a panic breathing into a paper bag, you will see the relevance of breathing. The over pollution of the lungs or the inability to breathe correctly can contribute to high blood pressure and the stress that goes along with it.

Thus, breathing correctly is central to good health.

Childhood problems can also play a part in developing stress through the development of self-esteem issues. Even alcohol consumption is seen as being a major factor in a person developing tensions and stress. Tension and stress can also arise because of circumstances beyond their control. Even the high flying businessman leaves himself open to health risks because he puts his work before his own state of health. Meditation can help him to focus and to be successful at the same time. It can also give him the rest that he needs in order to perform.

There are many causes of stress. The speed of life, the expectations of others and the expectations of self can all contribute. There are those who are stressed or depressed simply because of self-esteem issues that have their roots in the life experience of the individual. Stress isn't something with a cause that is easy to pinpoint, though the Anxiety and Depression Association of America quotes that the US spends over $43 billion a year on anxiety related treatments. Now that's a huge amount and pinpoints the vastness of the problem in just one country. Worldwide, that number is multiplied by many other statistics, meaning that stress is a vast cause of illness and wear on the body.

Q: Is meditation difficult to perform?

A: No. Meditation is very easy to perform. You just have to find a quiet place and have sufficient time to concentrate on your meditation practice. People think that meditation is hard to perform because of the images they see of people sitting in the Lotus position. It is not necessary to sit in this position to practice meditation. The important element is that you are comfortable and able to relax during your meditation session. Simply sitting in a chair is enough to relax and practice meditation, so don't think that complicated positions are needed in order to achieve the perfect position for mediation. Still others prefer to meditate in a horizontal position. Yes, that's right, you can lay down to meditate if you would like. Pretty much anywhere that

17

is comfortable will work for meditation purposes.

The correct process of meditating is explained in chapter 4 and you will learn the variances so that you can choose the system of meditation that you believe suits your own abilities and needs.

Q: Is it time consuming?

A: No. You can set your own time for meditation. Although the standard practice is to perform it for a minimum of 15 minutes per day, it is completely up to you to set the time. There are forms of meditation that only take minutes as well.

You can perform meditation for as little as 5 minutes or even as much as 30 minutes a day. You can also do it in two sittings, e.g. 15 minutes in the morning and 15 in the evening. Meditation can be done anywhere including your office, provided that the chosen place is sufficiently calm and that you are uninterrupted during your practice.

It might take a little more time for the effects to be felt if you do a 5-minute routine but it will definitely work and you will feel that your meditation is helpful. In the park, at lunchtime, you may not even be aware of people meditating. Such is the variety of meditation methods that the man on the park bench could be using his lunch break to get up close and personal with himself through mindful meditation.

The most important part of meditation is to ensure that you can perform it without wearing yourself out. Do not underestimate how much mental effort focusing takes. The point is to meditate until you feel refreshed, not exhausted.

Q: Will it require me to resort to contortions?

A: No. Unlike exercise and yoga, you will not have to twist your body or get into any positions that you find uncomfortable. There is little to no movement involved in meditation. You are not required to exercise in any physical way when meditating. Meditation is relaxation and thus all you will need to do is to be seated and exercise the mind, rather than the body. The only time that you may use physical exercise is if you are training in yoga and use meditation as part of your routine.

The effort that is exerted during meditation is completely mental. However, if you overdo your meditation exercises, you may feel physically drained as an after effect. The energy required to push external thoughts from your mind and focus on one specific thing can wear you out over time.

It is important that you are seated comfortably during meditation. Meditation is more exercise for the mind than it is for any other part of the body.

It is a mental exercise routine that will not require you to move around. The only type of meditation that involves movement is that which is classed as walking meditation, though this is used by people who find it an easier method than staying in one place and does not suit everyone. Think of meditation as relaxation from life. It is exercise for the mind rather than the body.

Q: Is it really effective?

A: Yes. Meditation is extremely effective in helping you cut down on your stress. It is, in fact, much more effective in helping you beat your tension in comparison to other activities such as exercising. Mentally training your brain to keep the stress out can help you better than trying to prevent it by avoidance. The former is more pragmatic as opposed to the latter. It works as a system to help you beat stress and may even help you to eliminate having to take very invasive medication, although you will need to check with your health practitioner before cutting out any medication prescribed. The sense of well-being that you will experience once you have mastered the technique of meditation will help you to overcome the bad habits of a lifetime and become very much more at peace in your life.

The level of its efficiency may differ from person to person but the effects will be visible within a few days of starting the routine. Even if it takes you longer, the beneficial effects of meditation are well established and the eventual success you experience will be life changing.

Science has proven that those who practice meditation on a regular basis have a lower blood pressure than people who do not. This is because they can avoid the feeling of stress, even in stressful situations.

Q: Is age a factor?

A: Yes and no. Although meditation can be safely followed by anybody of any age, it is better if children undertake it with adult supervision. And since most children do not feel stressed, they might not need it as much as adults. It can help students who are going through examinations. It can help kids who do feel stress and are unable to relax, though professional instruction may be the answer if there is any communication problem between the child and the parent or the child and peers. This gives the child a chance to experience personal space for relaxation.

Children who have trouble focusing, like kids with ADHD, tend to benefit from meditation more than children who do not suffer from a disorder like this. Studies have proven that children with ADHD benefit greatly from exercises like meditation. However, you have to ensure that your child understands the concept of meditation before you allow them to perform the exercises on their own.

However, meditation can be undertaken by students that are feeling the pressures of studies and they can safely practice meditation. They will feel more relaxed and will be better able to better concentrate on their studies. Thus, university campuses may run meditation courses for students and these would be worthwhile following because they help the student to feel less pressured and to feel more capable, thus helping the teen with their studies.

MEDITATION

As far as age goes, there is no higher limit as far as age is concerned. In fact, people of all ages enjoy it immensely. Older people find that it helps them with physical problems as well as psychological ones as it gives them the chance to exercise the respiratory system correctly and take advantage of the relaxation it affords them. It also helps elderly people to take control of their blood pressure, which in turn can help their overall general health state. That's an important tool to use against the process of aging.

CHAPTER 2

Meditation in General

Mediation is one of the most natural remedies known to man. It is a time that you can take and allow your body to heal itself through deep breathing and re-oxygenation. The more oxygen your cells and muscles receive, the better off they are when it comes to regenerating healthy cells. Your body will thank you greatly and will heal a lot faster through mediation than it will through traditional medicine.

It is important to realize that mediation is not a replacement for modern medicine but more of an assistance to the current medication regimen you currently have, at least until your doctor determines that it is safe to quit taking your medication.

Let your doctor know that you are practicing meditation and what your goals are. They will monitor your condition to determine when it is safe to reduce your medication or even take you off of your medication if you have learned to control your blood pressure or heart problem enough to be off of your medication.

How Meditation Can Change Your Life

Is it accurate to say that you are experiencing anxiety in your life or stress over your physical, mental or in other words your health? Is it true that you are wishing that you carry on with your life without anxiety and tension? Do you just want to live a life with a considerable amount of peace and harmony?

Anxiety is one of the worst mental disorders that you can suffer from. It feels as though the condition swallows your entire life and slowly envelops your entire being. You cannot go out to places with large groups of people or you feel overwhelmed at the smallest of glitches in your day. Meditation can help you learn to control your anxiety and your frustration that is associated with it. The fact that there is an exercise that can help you deal with anxiety without leaving you to feel drugged and sluggish is a relief in itself. You can finally take back control of your life.

You don't need to stress any longer in the light of the fact that numerous individuals have experienced through very similar experience in their lives and however that it is shockingly was better to them to die.

You may be focused on working for extended periods consistently that additionally represent a ton of anxiety to you. You may be focused on in light of the fact that you have a family that obliges you to have time with them, yet this is impractical in light of your employment. What's more, you may have advances, educational cost expenses, doctor's visit expenses, duties to pay and many debts that you need to pay.

When you fall under such as circumstance, you will be concentrating more on the most proficient method to make things work out, yet you will still need time for yourself. At the point when you are lying on your bed, your heart would start to beat so fast because of anxiety and have abnormal state of stress. This will happen in light of the fact that you are stressing over your children, charges, health, marriage and your general sanity.

Your health will be a noteworthy issue and you will at feel tired all the time. You may end up putting on a significant measure of weight, have harming back torment. You will understand that even by going up the stairs you will get tired and maybe a shortness of breath. Generally speaking, you will feel that everything in your life has broken apart.

You stress yourself about things, yet you may not realize what to do. You may choose to visit your gym class; in an attempt to lose weight, purchase a home practice machine and different projects to help you deal with your time. The best frustrations may come when you understand that you get comparable results after you attempt every one of the alternatives. At first they may work, yet you will most likely be unable to stick on any of them for a long time. The greater strategies offer a result that doesn't last for a very long time. Thus, you need to figure out how to change your life.

You have a long way to go, however certainly you will be unable to buy all books and you might likewise feel as though as you are reading so as you are cheating yourself by reading everything. In any case, as you are reading the books you will come over meditation that is the best process that will offer you awesome results. When you begin meditation, this will be the defining moment of your life. You ought not to expect in a moment results on the fact that this is a process that requires some serious energy and may be trying every now and then.

As you meditate, you will in any case be holding your most stressful job and other issues that may exists in present as well, however through meditation, you will feel more energetic and better. It won't help you resolve every one of the issues throughout your life, yet you will feel not so much stressed and become more relaxed. You will likewise have the capacity to focus on different things that will make you achieve spiritual, mental and physical health.

You can meditate at home and incorporate the right practice plan, for example, yoga, light walkout and walking. When you join such things with fitting eating routine, you will encounter a completely changed life in which you are in peace with your surroundings. Meditation is the process that will work for you.

How to Meditate

Meditating: breathing and watching your breath

Meditation has been proven to be a major benefit towards reducing anxiety. Minimize depression, lessen irritability, and boost the creativity and learning ability higher. Even in the beginning these are few of the benefits you will receive. There are some larger benefits that will help to increase vitality, reduce aging, reduced stress, reenergize, increase oxygen levels, and reduce stress and reduced blood pressure.

The Right way to Meditate

There are techniques that are possible in showing results instantly and they are as follows. Find a chair that is comfortable, sit in it and tense your body entirely with your eyes closed. Now let out a deep breath like a sigh and release the tension you held through your entire body. This will allow your body to feel where all the tension is held release and relax gently. This will allow your body to achieve great rest.

If your body is still experiencing some tenseness in areas than repeat the process making sure to tense the areas that are still tight. If a second time does not fix it, repeat a couple times until you feel completely relaxed. The more you repeat this, the more you will get used to you using this technique. You should always make time for meditation because it is good for you and if you don't repeat it you will not get the full effects of meditation that you may want to experience.

Breathing through your nose is better than breathing through your mouth so that your body receives more oxygen. This is caused by the diaphragm working more. You can test it by breathing through your mouth. You will notice that when you breathe through your mouth the breathing will be shallower. When you breathe through your nose you will notice that there is a further extension of the abdomen. When breathing through your nose the air will reach the farther parts of your lungs allowing more or all of your body parts to relax.

Keep your breathing steady and in a constant cycle. Focus on your breathing pattern as the air flows in and out of the nose. Make sure to keep focused on your breathing and if you get side tracked try to bring your focus back to your breathing. It will help you to meditate and relax giving you results that are positive. The more you do this the easier it will be to focus and the faster the meditation will help to provide a positive response in your body.

In the case where your mind is still completely active, you will need to push everything that is distracting you out of your way one at a time. There are different methods that you can use to make identification of distractions and elimination of distractions in your life possible. Move forward for six to ten minutes, or make one hundred deep breaths. After you have completed this cycle, open your eyes and sit comfortably without external distraction for a few minutes. This will ensure that you are completely refreshed and prepared to face the challenges of your day.

You have successfully carried out an effective session of meditation, yes it really is that simple!

Effects of Meditation

In the 1970's western researchers began to study impacts of speculation to people. Amid the studies they understood that sweat, heart rate and different emphasis signs lessened as middle person loose. Richard Davidson a researcher in the University of Badger State has been taking a gander at the long term of meditation. He got an invitation from the fourteenth Dalai Lama in 1992. He was welcomed to make representation of the brains of the Buddhist monks who were the first mediators on the planet. He later on moved to Bharat with generators, laptop computers, and EEG recording tools, and then he started to work on the ongoing project. Meanwhile in the modern days, the monks move to his WI lab to watch some exasperating visual pictures on the fact that EEGs take records of the reactions to know how their regulation aroused responses.

Any type of movement aids in making of new pathways and makes a few sections of the brain stronger. According to what Stephen Kosslyn said this fits into the entire neuroscience literature of professionalism. It regards take note of that when you do something for a quarter century eight hours for each day, you create something other than what's expected in your mind, which the individuals who don't do anything won't have. Monks were able to make three types of meditation which incorporate:

- Mediation that includes focusing on one particular object for quite a while.

- Cultivation by considering circumstances that cause outrage and modify the feeling into more empathy encounters

- Open presence that includes knowing every one of the feelings, musings and impressions that are available without responding to them in any case.

By getting to understand what was on the monks' mind, Richard Davidson chose to know the impacts it has on amateurs. He made a cogitation including forty one workers close to a biotech firm in River Wisconsin. Twenty-five of them edified care which is an accent minimizing shape that supports mindfulness that is nonjudgmental of the present circumstances as taught by Jon Kabat Zinn.

They took an interest in a seven hours retreat and week after week classes. Amid the two month week period, they were told to thoroughly consider for 60 minutes each. The estimations of the brain were taken before the directions were given, at the staying two months and four months after the retreat. The estimations taken demonstrated that increased substantial process in the frontal area of the nous that is situated on the left. This is part that is connected with low anxiety levels and state office that is decidedly energized. What's more, toward the end of the eight weeks, the members and sixteen controls got influenza shots to look at their reaction to invulnerable. Specialists likewise took test of blood from each of them every month and two months after they were infused. The outcomes demonstrated that the individuals who meditated had high number of antibodies against infection that cause influenza contrasted with the individuals who did not meditate. This demonstrated that contemplation makes the body more stable and have the capacity to battle against illness creating organisms. Along these lines, on the off chance that you have never considered meditation, this is the correct time to do as such and get the advantages included.

Why You Need to Meditate

There are countless side effects to meditation and all positive. Demonstrations have been studied on meditation and those who do regularly reduce need for rest, stress and illness.

The best reason that compels those who meditate to do so is the process itself. Meditation is amazing and the end result is not the best part it's the actual meditation itself that is sublime. During meditation you are carried away to tranquil awareness and contentment and not just when you are finished. This is a continuous cycle that you can repeat any time you need to relax and the more you do it the better you will feel.

Now of days we constantly experience stress through our daily lives. This stress is brought on by noise pollution, television, angry and envious people and arguments. The enlightening energy and internal reservoir of cleansing power that resides deep inside ourselves can be tapped into through meditation. This can help to reverse the effects of the enormous, negative, distress that overwhelms us daily.

In the past there was an abundance of nature such as trees, streams, and other natural occurrences. There were daily routines and rituals that were followed on a regular basis. There were not as many disturbances in the universe, like artificial sound vibrations from telephones, machinery and computers. Overall, the stresses of from the various complexities of urban industrial life did not exist. People enjoyed the sound of water, the gentle hum of the wind, the beauty of the sky and the stars. They enjoyed the true sounds and smells from the earth. Life had a natural tempo as people planted seeds, nurtured them into food and observed the given cycles of nature. They felt a connection to the earth directly. Now, everything we put into our bodies comes from a factory. We have completely divorced nature and our organic lifestyle.

Meditation allows us a great way to reenter the natural rhythms and aesthetics by closing out the unnatural world around us and rid our bodies of artificial stress that gathers and builds up in our lives.

The best part is that meditation cost absolutely nothing has absolutely no harmful effects. It does not add calories to your diet and it does not add any adverse chemicals either. It is not addictive and it does not have the same negative effects as drugs or alcohol, which most people use to unwind from their day. However, it has been proven that meditation provides a higher sense of wellbeing and practitioners have proven effects of mediation can be compared to a natural "high."

The human body is a complex machine and the human brain produces natural chemicals that are thousands of times more powerful than pharmaceuticals or narcotics. As a person medicates, the body secretes hormones that allow you to feel better and provide a rush of energy that brings happiness. This is another of the amazing side effects of meditation that is worth mentioning.

Meditation provides different feelings to everyone. Some use it in place of therapy or seeing a psychologist. Others find it a valuable tool to boost their sports performance or work performance. Yet others use it to boost their memory and expand their mental functions.

It has also been proven that meditation gives us a stronger and more sustainable vigor, sexual energy and calm feeling. It also provides restfulness that is conducive to exceptionally refreshing sleep.

Mediation Relaxing the Body and the Mind

Meditation is a condition of being centered on a certain idea and includes the "Quieting the mind", as you think internally, coming about to a more casual and cool feeling. This relaxation system can help a man add to his identity through mental order and also support his spiritual health by communing with God.

30

MEDITATION

Generally connected with some old eastern religions going back a few centuries, meditation has been assimilated in western society by means of spiritual practices and therapeutic treatments that concentrate on various types of recuperating with the assistance of the psyche and the inner energy.

As said by Dr. Borysenko, creator of 'Mending the Body, Mending the Mind', "...through meditation, we figure out how to get to the relaxing reaction (the physiological reaction inspired by meditation) and we turn out to be more mindful of the brain and the way our demeanor produces stress." He trusts that through meditation, one can likewise reach the "inner physician" and permit the body's own inner wisdom to be heard.

In Taoism, the mind that controls and feels emotions is controlled by the "Fire" energy of the heart. Unrestrained, this Fire energy sends its flares upward and becomes able wastefully to burn up the energy and also smothers the mind. On the other hand, the mind that controls intent, or will power, is controlled by the Water energy of the human kidneys. Without any type of direction, the "Water" energy is being flushed down the sexual organ that drains the essence and also spirit. Anyway, when you practice meditation, these flows of Water and Fire energies are now being reversed. The Water energy is now being drawn up to the head, through the center of these channels, while the Fire energy that comes from the heart is being drawn down into the lowest part of the Elixir Field in the abdomen, Where the energy is being refined as well as being transformed. This process lets the mind that controls intent, which is Water, to be able to provide a soothing and relaxing effect all over the mind that controls emotions, which is Fire. Hence, meditation relaxation happens.

During nowadays, where in the world we live in there is so much chaos and negativism brought by mans who are going after wealth and power, many were victims to stress and anxiety, no need to also mention a lot of medical conditions like cardiovascular and respiratory diseases.

31

MEDITATION

Meditation relaxation covers the whole of the body and mind. It really benefiting in providing relief to the people who are suffering from anxiety disorders because it allows the person to be able to experience relaxation and it is also able to release negative energies stored in the body, letting you acquire a totally different type of healing which is not available using only medications. But this strategy is a not easy to learn, and it needs to be learned properly. Whenever you are training on the art of amazing mediation you need to make sure that there are no distractions.

A yoga meditation key principle in this process is attention and breathing. These two principles can work together naturally and perfectly in allowing the body to reach its full relaxation and mind it, as well as the mind.

There are times when the mind is restless that it could not keep itself from getting distracted and have the tendency to open the eyes or make unnecessary movements during the process. What some practitioners do is to make use of external device or stimulus like music or visual support to get to that state of relaxation. However, to train the mind means not relying on this external technique but directly working in the mind itself.

If you are interested in training the restless mind, you need to firstly acknowledge it as restless and it doesn't really happen in the easy way, which you are expecting it. Make sure that you give your mind something to do, something that is totally internal and real, not something that is external or a part of a fantasy. Make sure you focus on what is within the body and also please do not create something that doesn't actually exist in real. That is what makes yoga meditation so amazing. So, whether your goal is to get rid of the stress you have, cure illness or gaining a higher level of spiritual connection, Yoga meditation is the best for all that as well as other relaxation strategies that can help you find the healing power you need or acquire, all that by only training your mind how to reach the power of the inner being in you.

MEDITATION

The Healing Wonders of Meditation

Meditation is an ancient practice common among religions for its spiritual enlightenment and healing. It has been proven and is accepted as an alternative therapy known as "mind-body medicine."

Meditation has been found more and more through the years for its effectiveness to improve heart health, ease chronic pain, relieve anxiety and stress, boost immunity and mood, and resolve pregnancy problems. Meditation is being prescribed by doctors to help improve exercise performance for angina patients; help lower blood pressure; relieve insomnia; and help people to control their asthma and breathe more easily. Meditation can be used as a simple and safe way to stabilize a person's emotional, physical, and mental well being.

According to cardiologist Herbert Benson, MD: "Any condition that's caused or worsened by stress can be alleviated through meditation." At Harvard Medical School's Beth Israel Deaconess Medical Center the Mind/Body's founder is Benson. Benson says that meditation can help to induce relaxation and help lower blood pressure, decrease metabolism, and improve breathing, heart rate, and brain waves. A person's body's muscles will start to drain away the tightness and tension from the muscles when it receives a quiet message.

Meditation has been proven to really work when a brain scan (or Magnetic Resonance Imaging, or MRI) was performed on people who have meditated. These scans show and activity increase in the areas of the brain that control heart rate and metabolism. There have been studies through Buddhist monks that show long-lasting changes to activity in the brain involving working memory, attention, conscious perception and learning.

Meditation is a easy task in itself but difficult to control in its entirety. It must be practiced to develop the ability to ignore distraction of the surrounding and your thoughts along with focusing on your breathing patterns. At the end of meditating a mantra, phrase or word is usually chanted to help with the biological response to help in relaxation. Repetition is soothing and the key to meditation. The more we practice the easier the meditative state will come to us and the more we will relax. Meditating multiple times a day can help to keep our day relaxed and more stress free through the entire day.

Benefits of Meditation

Heart Health: There have been many studies that show practicing meditation can help significantly with reducing high blood pressure. Studies have been conducted at the College of Maharishi Vedic Medicine in Fairield, Iowa, that show the heart rate in black adults were lowered significantly with meditation. There have also been studies conducted on teenagers by the American Journal of Hypertension showing that two sessions of meditation for 15 minutes over a period of four months can help to lower their blood pressure by a few points.

Immune Booster: Meditation has been studied with Psychosomatic Medicine for its effect on immune function. It has shown to help in warding off infections and illness. In a group of volunteers who meditated for 8 weeks and those who didn't they were given flu shots. When they checked blood tests in the group that meditated it had shown that they produced antibodies in higher levels against the flu virus.

Women's Health: It has shown that breastfeeding, infertility problems, and Premenstrual syndrome (PMS) in those who meditate regularly have been improved. There was a study, PMS symptoms in women who meditated subsided by 58%. There was also a study that shows women who meditate have less intense hot flashes. Anxiety, fatigue and depression in women struggling with their infertility were decreased by those who meditated for 10 weeks. 34% of those who did the meditation became pregnant in the first six months. Mothers were able to double their milk production when they meditated on a flow of milk from their breasts.

MEDITATION

Meditation Enhances Brain Activity

A brain activity that was shown to be higher in those that meditates regularly. This is shown through activity know as gamma waves, which are the happiness and learning centers of the brain. Memory, attention, conscious perception and learning are all part of the mental process shown through gamma waves.

Meditation is being considered by health care providers and being integrated as a key element for the health program. Also if you are having a hard time getting started into a state of meditation there are classes you can enroll in. They can show you may practices that will help you to start the relaxation process that is beneficial. This can be achieved through yoga, meditation, or prayer. Studies are showing that meditation is just as good as any other alternative therapies.

Positive Thought Process

Your negative or positive attitude is completely up to you. Your mind set is created by you. You are the one who makes the decisions such as who your friends are, the environment you live in or the attitude you have.

Your mind is just like a computer. It absorbs the data around it and grows with what you take in. A lot of people think that their mind is not under their control. In all reality this is a misjudgment because of surrounding negativity. This negativity is found in the environment or influence from others unconstructive ideas.

Your brain is just like a computer. When infected with bad data such as a virus to a computer you need to notice it as soon as possible so that it does not spread through your mind. This bad negative data can be passed around to your friends or other people around you. So in this way you are spreading energy that is negative to everyone else like a flu.

MEDITATION

You yourself are like a farmer. You also have the ability to help nourish the information or positive thoughts that your mind grows with. Just like a field that grows with no help or nourishment it will not be as abundant and healthy as a field that does have positive input and care.

This works the same way for our mind and the energy it grows with.

You are the deciding factor to the quality of information you take in such as reading eBooks, books, CD's, DVD's, courses, lectures, seminars, and workshops. This information will help to improve your positive mind-set.

You cannot stop at just taking in positive information. You also need to reinforce your energy by continuously adding to the energy you take in. Never stop feeding on good thoughts and energies. Help your mind to grow like the farmer helps his crops by giving his crops water and fertilizer. Just remember you still have to block out the negative information. Just like any garden you have to keep at it constantly or negativity will continue to grow and break its way through. Meditation is one of the ways we can help to focus on the energy we take in and increase our thought process about what is positive and negative.

Meditation is focusing on a thought, object, task or any other obstacle you may come across to make a good, healthy decision.

Meditation makes us slow down and observe the positive and negative sides to a problem so that we can learn and grow to continue to make the right decisions. It will also help with taking negative issues and turn them into positive experiences to learn by. You will help to create a positive mindset to set you forward in your life. The outcome will be reaching your goals, making new friends, develop a strong willed spirit, and help you to handle problems more easily.

When you remember the accomplishments you made in the past it gives you a good feeling of empowerment to continue moving forward. The ability to have these feelings are inside all of us and create the formula that drives us to be successful, but it is up to you to bring the formula together for your positive mindset. There is a huge majority out there that will not take action to push forward and be positive.

Use meditation to settle your mind and soul and help you to make the decision to get out from the everyday pack of people and push ahead with action and education.

CHAPTER 3

Benefits of Meditation

"If you want to conquer the anxieties of life, live in the moment, live in the breath."

Amit Ray

Meditation has several benefits to the body. These benefits encompass both the mental and physical aspects of a human being.

These aspects are mentioned in this chapter, though there are other ways in which meditation helps which are covered in other chapters of this book.

Physical Benefits of Meditation

Blood pressure

One of the biggest benefits of meditation is that it helps in cutting down on high levels of blood pressure some people experience, and also helps in maintaining a normal level when meditation practice becomes regular. Blood pressure is the main culprit that causes people to develop some of the most fatal diseases in the world including heart disease and hypertension. Although it might take some time for people to develop high blood pressure, its slow build up can go unnoticed for a long time. Thus, prevention is better than seeking a cure. If the blood pressure is controlled by a healthy lifestyle and meditation, then there won't be the need to face the many of the problems that are associated with high blood pressure. That makes it a win-win situation.

MEDITATION

Simply by using meditation, you are going to be able to calm yourself through the concentration on your breathing. Often the pace at which you are breathing will determine how hard your heart is beating. If you are breathing really quickly, then your heart is more likely to be pumping faster and your blood pressure is going to be higher. There are a variety of reasons why you might have a higher heart rate including stress, but the breathing techniques used in meditation will be able to relax you and get your blood pressure down at the same time.

Since people who suffer stress leave themselves prone to heart disease, this can only be seen as a boost to the body. Meditation makes you mindful and thus you are aware of your body's needs and also aware of any need to slow down to help the blood pressure return to normal without the use of medications. This is indeed a boost because it means that you won't have to suffer the side effects of medications either.

Joints

Meditation helps in keeping all parts of the body in good shape. Among these body parts are the various joints in the body. The brain releases chemicals that help to keep them lubricated and therefore several diseases related to joints such as arthritis can be kept at bay. It is especially useful in older people and those who have a predisposition towards arthritic conditions. If you know, for example, that relatives have suffered from arthritis, meditation will help you to control the onset in your particular case.

It also helps in fighting carpel tunnel syndrome, which is a very common joint related disease amongst youth owing to the amount of time that they spend typing on their computer keyboards and cellphone keypads. The anti-inflammatory effect of relaxation helps considerably those who suffer these problems and so the relaxation gained from meditation will help you if you suffer. The repetitive motion used during this technological communication may be something that should be seen as a cause of carpel tunnel syndrome and it may be better to change your lifestyle to help you to avoid it as well.

MEDITATION

Immunity

Regular meditation can help in keeping the body extremely fit and healthy. The mind controls the functioning of the body to a very large extent and in ways that are hard to imagine.

It will promote the release of antioxidants that will help fight the free radicals in cells, which can cause cancers. It also helps in stimulating the Kupffer cells in the liver, which are the body's first line of defense against disease.

Regular meditation can help the body develop a resistance to common diseases such as coughs and colds and also help prevent contagious diseases from affecting the body. This can be more effective than using cold remedies or taking in a lot of vitamin C. The best part is that you will not have to spend a lot of time on meditation for it to have effect. Fifteen minutes or so is usually enough to reap the benefits that you are looking for. The immune system is a very important part of human biology and if you can keep this healthy, you are half way to achieving the health benefits and precautionary measures to shield off disease. The mind is excessively powerful, as is thought, but when you consider concentrated thought, such as used in meditation, the power is increased.

Energy levels

Regular meditating can help in maintaining high levels of energy. When a person breathes rapidly, he/she inhales a lot of fresh oxygen. This oxygen helps in rejuvenating every single cell in the body. When cells feel rejuvenated, they expand and can hold more energy giving nutrients such as carbohydrates.

Along with a balanced diet, a person can easily add several years to their age and, in fact, reverse the effects of aging and start to appear much younger. Several celebrities undertake meditation for this purpose and try to avoid going under the knife as much as possible.

41

MEDITATION

Aches and pains

As was said earlier, the mind controls the body to a very large extent. It takes care of all the functioning of the body and also helps in keeping the body fit and healthy. If a person has a mind full of tension and worries then he/ she is sure to develop a headache or other potential symptoms of a negative nature. With migraine being one of the most common types of diseases, it is even more important for people to relax and take up meditation to avoid this from happening.

Regular meditation can help in keeping muscle pains, joint aches, joint swellings etc. at bay. It can also help in reducing existing aches and pains.

Age reversal effects

By far one the greatest and most beneficial effects of meditation is the ability to make you feel younger. If you don't believe that, then hear what is said by the experts. Dharma Singh Khalsa, who is a leading expert on Alzheimer's disease research, states:

"Meditation lowers blood pressure and other markers of aging including MVO2 or oxygen demand. It enhances psychological well-being, perhaps the most significant determinate of telomere length (telomeres are the end cap of our DNA), which is a very important marker of aging and longevity: longer telomeres = less illness + longer life."

That's a pretty powerful message to people who are thinking about meditation but who are not yet convinced of the benefits it can give them. Imagine feeling younger, imagine your body being able to withstand the process of aging in a more graceful way and you may indeed see that it's more powerful than other forms of natural medicine in achieving what it sets out to do.

MEDITATION

Mental Benefits of Meditation

Tensions can be reduced

When a person meditates, he/ she automatically starts to control the mind in a much better way. Once the mind is trained, it can automatically keep tension out and maintain a calm state of mind. As soon as it realizes that there is a source of tension, then it automatically sends the brain into a state of conscious control. That's the way that people who meditate are able to control the way that they react to given stimuli. Meditation helps them to focus elsewhere and thus avoid the negative effects of situations that can be turned into positive learning experiences. This is also why people who meditate regularly rarely have blood pressure problems or heart conditions. The ones that do have these conditions manage their condition easily because their brain can control their level of stress unlike the typical human brain.

The subconscious then prepares itself to take problems head on and deals with them to the fullest capacity. In the process, it also develops a resistance and prevents future attacks. Regular meditation is therefore said to be extremely beneficial in beating everyday tensions and helping people to lead a calmer life. Given the power of meditation, it's not surprising that the body is better able to deal with the harsh blows that life may aim at it. No one can pretend that bad things don't happen, but it prepares the body and makes it better able to deal with bad events or negative influences.

Anxiety prevention

Anxiety is a state of mind that is brought on by regular tension. Several days of tension and stress can cause anxiety to occur and the best way to prevent it is by practicing meditation.

Meditation can, in fact, root out anxiety, as it will not at all allow you to undergo stress in the first place. And so, when stress is left out of the picture, the person will automatically not develop any anxiety or a reaction to the stress that is associated with a given situation. With a few minutes spent on a daily basis to undertake meditation, a person can easily remedy his/ her anxiety levels. There have been a multitude of people who have reversed chronic anxiety disorders using meditation as the primary treatment for their disorder.

How this works is that through meditation, a human being is better able to control emotions that may trigger anxiety attacks. Thus, with these emotions being controlled, it's unlikely that the stage of anxiety will be reached, since the mind will know how to deal with the problems that may lead to that state where anxiety takes over.

Optimism promotion

A positive attitude is extremely important in life. If a person only thinks negative thoughts then he/ she is bound to experience tension and stress. In order to beat stress, it is important to think positively no matter what the situation. People who suffer from major diseases such as cancer are taught that positive attitude and thinking will help them to go through the terrible ordeal and to come out of the other side feeling better. Positive attitude heals, and is thus something that all people should try to adopt as a generally healthy attitude helps healing. Negativity can do the opposite, so that all that you gain from your meditation will help to optimize your feeling of being at peace with the world and kill off those feelings of pessimism.

And to think positively, it is important to meditate and train the mind on a regular basis. It is important to gain a control over the mind and alter the train of thought. This way, you are better able to deal with stress and all of the pessimism that goes with it. A person practicing meditation on a regular basis will start to develop optimism and stop having negative thoughts and feelings that will directly affect their lives in a positive manner.

MEDITATION

Emotional stability

Life has become extremely unpredictable these days and there are just so many relationships to manage that we often find ourselves having to deal with emotional instability. There are so many ups and downs in life that can cause stress and emotional disturbances. Meditation helps you to control that element in your life.

It is the era of divorce, and that means that emotional stability will be affected. With worry about children, possessions and all the trappings of life, it's no wonder that people fall into the trap of emotional instability. However, meditation helps them to center their thoughts and to get beyond all of these events with a real strength that is able to help them to think over the problems that may otherwise have been too difficult to face. It strengthens the resolve and helps people to look from a distance at problems that have become too close, thus finding solutions that take into account everyone who is involved in the situation.

The simple answer to the question of emotional instability is meditation not medication. With meditation, you can take control of your emotions. You can control how you feel in certain situations and also move away from a situation when you recognize it to be detrimental. You will turn into a more forgiving person and stop getting so angry about life. In fact, meditation helps you to see the picture from all sides and to balance and weigh your decisions in a much clearer manner. It also helps you to feel empathy and humility and these are important aspects when considering your own mental fragility. Most people are fragile in bad situations because they allow their emotions to rule their physical state. However, with meditation on a regular basis, the balance is addressed and progress is made that diverts attention away from instability to a place of security.

MEDITATION

Intelligence can be improved

With meditation, you can easily increase your memory power. And when you increase your memory power, you will be able to remember things better and use this to your own benefit. The trouble is that people stop learning because they close off their minds to new ideas. Meditation helps you to remain open at all times and that helps you in turn to become a much more complete human being. You see things differently and with a clarity that helps you to retain information.

You will feel like a smarter person and start to have better conversations with people. You will start making better decisions that will help you garner more success and also aid in building a better rapport with your family and friends. The relationship between meditation and understanding others is well known, because meditation makes you stop in your tracks and think about your next action, instead of making many of the mistakes that people make by not giving a situation sufficient thought.

You may be surprised at what you can achieve, because instead of letting life pass you by, you are stopping to greet it and to see all the opportunities that pass your way, rather than being too busy to notice them. You also garner much intelligence from observation and people who do not find the time to observe are missing out on the opportunity to improve who they are and how they see the world. This is all part of intelligence. It isn't just about book learning. It's about being able to form relationships with those around you and doing so in a very humane, intelligent and understanding way.

The Power of Your Subconscious Mind

Scientists say that we only use approximately 10 % of our minds. The other 90% is being wasted. Think of it in this manner, what would happen if you only used 10% of your salary? You survive on 10% of the money that you make? For most people the answer to this question is no.

MEDITATION

What about 10% of the food you eat on a daily basis? Or only 80 minutes of sleep out of that 8 hours that is recommended. Your life would be complete chaos. Imagine living off of only 10% of the oxygen that you take in everyday? Just the thought of this is petrifying!

So if we can't life using 10% of anything else, why would we settle for using only 10% of our brain?

Are you living the life that you want? Actually living life on your terms and not the terms that the universe had dealt you? While making your life better may seem like a fairytale, think about the potential you have if you begin unlocking pieces of your mind that you are not using right now. Meditation allows you to focus and use the power of your subconscious to take over and to do things that you never dreamed possible. Including heal your mind and body.

It has been proven scientifically that those who meditate live a life filled with more harmony, wealth, health, joy and success. If you do not have these things yet, it is not your fault. You were never taught how to use your mind correctly and neither were your ancestors.

The moment you picked up this book, everything that happened before that point became your past. Your subconscious now does what you tell it to. Want to prove it? Look at the clock before you go to sleep tonight and tell your subconscious to wake you up at 7:00 am. I bet that within a few minutes of 7:00 am, your eyes will pop open.

During meditation you have the power to tell your subconscious what it is. Not what it wants to be. You can tell your subconscious to listen to you. It is going to become more efficient at work and it is going to get you the raise you have wanted for the last few years. You are going to start living healthier and become a healthier person.

While you are doing this, use the power of affirmation, or the power of convincing yourself that it is possible to become exactly what you want to be. Tell yourself what you are in a positive way and this is what you will become.

CHAPTER 4

Types of Meditation

"The mind can go in a thousand directions, but on this beautiful path, I walk in peace. With each step, the wind blows, with each step, a flower blooms."

Thích Nhất Hạnh

When people mention meditation, often people think about the sight of a person sitting with folded legs and chanting "om." That is mainly because of how meditation is projected in the media. But meditation is not limited to just that kind of activity. There are many types of meditation practices that a person can adopt and when you know the different types, you can choose the one that best suit your needs. Some people try all the different types of meditation in order to find the most suitable. You never know, you may find that there is a system of meditation that suits you better than all others. Look through the different types because if you can find one that fits your lifestyle, this will benefit you. There is so much to gain from meditation and you can only find out how much by taking part. Once you do, it's unlikely that you will look back to a time when meditation was not part of your life.

The various types of meditation practices along with their methods are explained below in detail so that you can work out which fits with your needs or your lifestyle.

MEDITATION

Traditional meditation

Also known as transcendental meditation, this form is popular for its simplicity and extreme effectiveness. This form of meditation is extensively practiced all over the world and is said to be one of the most effective methods. This meditation is best performed every day and preferably during the early morning hours before the world begins to become busy. When you practice this form of meditation in the morning, you are allowing your body the chance to rejuvenate the way that it needs to. You can give yourself some extra energy in order to get through the day feeling more relaxed and without the usual stresses that you might be used to dealing with.

This form of meditation is probably the most popular form with the western world although mindful meditation is beginning to become every bit as popular with people who suffer from stress. Its worthwhile checking out both styles of meditation as each have their merits. Traditional meditation is likely to that which is easier to learn in a group situation or one on one with an instructor. Of course, you can learn to do this yourself at home but do read the instructions carefully. The benefit of doing meditation as part of a group is that others give you the incentive to carry on and achieve the different exercises taught, to maximize the benefit that you reap from the meditation.

How to perform:

To perform transcendental meditation, you must sit down and fold your legs. If you have the capacity to, then you can place both your heels on the opposite thigh, as shown in the page, by interlocking your legs (this is a very advanced form and you might want to exercise caution). Stretch out your hands and place the back of your hands on the knee. Take a deep breath and hold it for a couple of seconds. Slowly release and close your eyes as you do.

MEDITATION

Image: Creative Commons Attribution: Jemasty

The position shown in the image is the lotus position and is a standard position for meditation, although some people may find this a little awkward at first. This is because tucking your legs into this position may not seem comfortable. If you do have circulation problems, you should talk to your instructor about positions that can be used until your body is a little more versatile. There is some good advice shown here about the different postures that a practitioner of meditation can use as an alternative, bearing in mind how hard it is to keep the feet in this position without practice. The half lotus may be a good alternative for a newcomer, although you should note that posture is of paramount important to meditation techniques and that the spine should always be kept in a straight position.

When you start to take in the next breath, chant a soothing word like "om" or any other word that will help you to stabilize your breathing and relax. The idea behind the "om" chant is that it gives the mind something central to concentrate on and helps you to avoid being distracted. Om doesn't have a meaning and thus it cannot take you off into a chain of thought, which is why a nonsense word is used.

Repeat for 5-15 minutes. You can start with 5 and then slowly increase to 15.

MEDITATION

Less advanced students will first be taught how to breathe correctly and will be encouraged to try the different positions until a suitable one is found which allows the body full stability as well as helping keep the posture straight. Usually this involves simply crossing the legs comfortably.

The benefits of traditional meditation

This method of meditation was practiced in India and it was found that the beneficial effects of this style of meditation take a while for a practitioner to feel. It takes practice because the stillness is not something that modern day people are accustomed to. It isn't merely a question of sitting in a certain position, breathing and using a chant. It's a question of inner focus and that's where people find this hard. Once you do master it, it will help your health, your mental aptitude and your concentration levels. Traditional meditation concentrates on the mantra or chant because it helps to take away concentration on worldly things, thus relaxing the mind and allowing it the benefit of the rest that it needs. Thus, it gives the body a chance to heal, to relax and thus slow down the blood pressure, help the immune system to repair itself and makes the body and mind feel at one with the world around it.

Breathing meditation

Also known as yoga meditation, breathing meditation causes a person to concentrate on his/ her breath. The breath has amazing powers and its true benefits can only be harnessed by a person if he/ she makes use of this type of practice. With this kind of meditation, you are going to learn how to breathe in and out to a certain rhythm, focusing only on the breaths that you are taking and nothing else. The breaths are able to help you to calm down because you will be able to focus on long slow breaths and you will be able to watch the tension melt away. It is also a good thing to concentrate on so that you are not focusing on anything else or getting distracted.

MEDITATION

Bear in mind that different exercises are useful in this method of meditation, since different breathing exercises hone in on areas of difficulty and help with certain problems, such as lack of concentration, anxiety levels, etc.

There are two types of breathing meditation practices with one being the pranayama and the other being Bhrastrika pranayama. Both of these types of meditation use the breathing exercises in conjunction with concentration on the breathing in and out. It's like exploring your body from the inside and will help you to be conscious of breathing correctly and using your diaphragm area in the right way.

How to perform:

To perform Pranayama, sit with your legs folded and hands stretched out. Now place your thumb on your right nostril and breathe in through your left nostril. Hold it for a couple of seconds before closing your left nostril with your index finger and exhaling through your right nostril. This may sound strange, but it's necessary to follow the flow of the breathing as you are doing this, thus becoming aware of the breath that you take, following it down from the nostril to the throat, from the throat to the lungs. When breathing out, you should be aware of the movement of your diaphragm and also of the breath escaping from the diaphragm area up through your body and out.

Repeat for 5-15 minutes. Remember to take it slowly for the first few days and then you can do it for a maximum of 30 minutes per day.

Have your eyes closed and concentrate on your lungs expanding and contracting. Feel the air flow into your body and be aware of its movement within the body at all times. It's not a case of just breathing; it's about living that breath. Just as in traditional meditation, the practitioner concentrates on the "om" the practitioner of this form of meditation concentrates on the very air that enters and leaves the body.

MEDITATION

To perform Bhrastrika pranayama, sit with a straight back and folded legs and allow your body to draw a breath and exhale. Concentrate again and take a deep breath.

Continue for 2-3 minutes. Remember that this is an advanced form of meditation and you must not do this for more than 5 minutes a day and on alternate days. If you overdo it then you might start feeling dizzy and might even pass out.

Note: Concentrating, used in this sense, means taking in the joy of the moment and that's a vital part of this form of meditation.

This form of meditation is common to those who practice yoga and a yoga teacher can talk you through the process and guide you in your endeavors to make breathing meditation part of your lifestyle.

Benefits of breathing meditation

The idea of this kind of meditation is that the link between the mind and the breathing creates a bridge. Being conscious of your breathing methods, you actually improve the way that the body takes in and expels air. Many people in this day and age have forgotten how to breathe correctly and do not give their bodies the chance to get sufficient oxygenation, thus making the body sluggish in its responses. This kind of meditation can sharpen the senses, make the practitioner more aware of caring of their body and make them a lot less likely to suffer from stress. Stress is often related to bad breathing practice coupled with emotional difficulties. By using this form of meditation, you are able to counter these problems and thus avoid stress or anxiety, which can become out of control.

Listen to your own breathing for a moment and even look at the way that you breathe. If you are not breathing through the nostrils, and many people don't, you may not be giving your body all the air that it needs for it to be fully efficient. Watch how you breathe out. Do you expel air from your lungs, your abdomen area? Be conscious of your breathing because breathing meditation can help you considerably to ward off illnesses and help the immune system to be more effective. It can also sharpen concentration and make you much more aware of your body and its current condition.

Heart rhythm meditation

As the name suggests, heart rhythm meditation deals with you following your heart's rhythm. This form of meditation is extremely popular owing to its effectiveness in bringing about an instant calm. You will have to work on controlling the heart rate that you have if you want this to be effective. If the heart is beating really quickly, this means that you are stressed out and have things that are weighing on your mind.

You need to be able to work on controlling how fast the heart is going so that you can do this effectively. A nice and steady heartbeat is ideal for your health but also in calming you down so that you are able to perform the other tasks that you need in your life without all of the stresses that can come from being anxious or worrying about other things.

How to perform this form of meditation:

To perform this type of meditation, sit with your legs folded and close your eyes. Now stretch your left hand out and fold your right palm. Place your folded fingers over your heart. Now draw in a deep breath and visualize the breath moving into your body and reaching your heart. As you feel your heart beat, visualize the fresh air cleansing your heart and your heart feeling the refreshment of the exercise. Now visualize all the bad air and toxins exiting your body.

Continue for a few minutes. It is ideal for you to perform this type of meditation for as long as is comfortable for you. Make sure that you are in an open-air atmosphere and there is pin drop silence.

MEDITATION

How heartbeat rhythm meditation helps

This form of meditation dates back as far as 8000 years. It is popularly used in Tai Chi because of its power to help practitioners to achieve better sleep. Sleep is the time when the body is doing the majority of its healing. In fact, while you sleep, the healing power of the body works making sure that you are in tiptop condition the next morning. That's why sleep is so important. Heart listening also enables you to have more energy during the day and thus use this to help your logical processes. It is used to help you hone in on your natural abilities and to feel the joy of living.

Kundalini meditation or Sahaja Yoga Meditation

Kundalini refers to a form of energy that is present inside everybody's body. Kundalini awakening is achieved by using the method of meditation, which is called Sahaja Yoga Meditation. Everybody is made up of 7 chakras or wheels that rotate and cause a person to be healthy. If there are blockages in these chakras then the person will face bad health and also suffer from tension and stress. This type of meditation practice will help in clearing the various blockages.

How to perform:

To perform this type of meditation, sit with your legs folded and your hands stretched out. Now visualize a ball of light to originate from your first chakra that is located behind the pubic bone. Now imagine that it is slowly moving to the second chakra, which is located in your stomach. It then moves to the third one located next to your heart. Then to the fourth one that is located in your throat. It then moves to the fifth one located in your temple, then to the sixth one that is located inside your brain. Finally, it pierces through your mind and goes through the aura, which is located above your head.

Do this for no more than 15 minutes a day.

MEDITATION

The benefits of this form of meditation

This form of meditation is associated with your spiritual well-being. This helps you to be closer to your origins and beliefs. Therefore, it is capable of bringing you great inner peace. People who feel this inner peace are less likely to suffer from stresses or from anxiety as the meditation teaches a certain amount of calm, which people can escape to instead of succumbing to stress.

Walking meditation

As the name suggests this form of meditation deals with performing meditation as you walk around. This form of meditation is said to not only help you exercise your mind but also allow you to attain a healthy body. The origin of this form of meditation is that it was used by The Buddha when he was looking for answers. What he found was that this form of meditation allowed him to be aware of his surroundings and to be at peace with them.

How to perform:

To perform this type of meditation, find a quiet area where you can walk around in circles. These circles need not be too big and can be made up of small turns. Now start walking around with your arms folded behind you. Every time that you place your right leg forward, you must draw in a breath and when you place your left leg forward, you must let your breath out.

If it feels too tiring to do so, then you can breathe in and out during every alternate step. You can also have a watch that will allow you to match the steps with its second hand although this way takes away from the original idea of walking meditation, in that if you use a stop watch, you will be more intent upon watching that than being aware of your surroundings. Thus if you can gauge the level of your breathing simply by trying to breathe in harmony with your movement, you will find this to be much more efficient. Another method instead of using the steps as a guide is to hold a meditation necklace and use the beads to indicate the in and out breaths.

The benefits of walking meditation

Walking meditation is a good practice for the deep thinker or those who find keeping still difficult. However, the goodness from this form of meditation comes from the concentration on the breathing and the awareness of your surroundings, though without using these as a distraction. It's very complex but what it does is make you feel an inner peace and understanding. Just as the Buddha established great understanding in order to write his findings on mindfulness.

Qi gong meditation

Qi gong is a traditional form of meditation technique that is said to have originated in China. It is said to be quite useful in calming down a person and clearing his/ her mind of problems. Qi gong is easy to perform and you can do it during any time of the day. This form of meditation is closely related to Kundalini and follows a similar pattern. This system of meditation will help you to focus your attention on specific things within your life, improving your approach to them.

How to perform:

To perform qi gong form of meditation, sit with your legs folded and your palms on your knees. Now imagine a ball of air originating from your first chakra and move to your fourth and then to your throat chakra. The same ball keeps moving up and down between these chakras and clears all blockages and allows the chakras to turn without any hindrance.

You can perform this meditation for 15 minutes and for a maximum of 30 minutes per day.

MEDITATION

How this form of meditation helps:

Qi gong helps you to be more focused and more focused people suffer less with emotional problems. They are able to see specific problems and find answers to them fairly easily because the meditation helps them to clear up their breathing, their awareness and their mental focus. It is also unlikely that people who practice this kind of meditation would suffer from stress or from depression, since it is geared toward positive energy.

Zazen meditation

The zazen form of meditation is designed for individuals who have not much time on their hands and are always rushing from one place to another. This form of meditation is best performed by those people who are looking for a very simple form of meditation and nothing as elaborate as concentrating on the breath, heartbeat or chakras.

How to perform:

To perform this meditation, the person must simply sit with the legs folded and relax. He/ she should stop all thought processes and think about absolutely nothing.

This can be done for as long as a person thinks he/ she can peacefully perform it without being affected by outside distractions and disturbances.

The value of this kind of meditation:

A still mind is a very peaceful one. If you can manage with silence to think of nothing at all, then you are stopping all the negative thoughts from getting in the way of spiritual and mental development and abilities. This may sound simple, although it takes a lot of practice for it to be beneficial. People are accustomed to living in a busy world, and silencing it or locking out the interference of the world will benefit practitioners because it frees the mind, even if temporarily, of worries and stresses. This, in turn, strengthens the emotional side of your character and also puts things into better perspective.

Trance based meditation

Trance based meditation is one where another person is required to help induce a trance. This technique is slightly advanced and is to be followed by those who are in an advanced state of anxiety. It may help to calm the nerves.

How to perform:

To perform this type of meditation, a person must get a professional hypnotist to hypnotize him/ her. This can be done in many ways and the trained hypnotist will recognize the best method to use once he/ she gets acquainted with you.

Just make sure that the person brings you back to consciousness after a set period of time. This kind of guided trance when performed by a professional only takes you into a medium trance. This is where your body is guided by their words. Your hands may feel heavy, your eyelids may also be heavy and when you awaken from the trance, you will feel a sense of wellbeing.

Light trance

To achieve this, you need to watch your own body and understand how it works. When you go to bed at night, just before you drop off to sleep, your body goes into a light trance. By observing this, you are able to replicate the effect. It is, in effect, a very light feeling where nothing worries you and where nothing really goes through your mind.

Trance meditation benefits

This can help an individual with anxiety problems and those who are seeking to find some kind of relaxation technique that works for them. In fact, the trance state in light form is that wonderful relaxing feeling of nothingness that overcomes all thoughts and allows you total relaxation. Since relaxation is extremely important to health, there are obvious benefits to your mental ability to cope, your state of tiredness and your ability to wake up fresh and be able to solve problems.

Guided visualization

This form of meditation can be very calming. It is easy to perform and can be undertaken at any time of the day. This kind of visualization is very powerful indeed and can help you to achieve your hopes and dreams, thus leaving you in a very happy state. Use this to reinforce positive thoughts and you will immediately reap the benefits.

How to perform:

To perform this type of meditation, you must assume a relaxing pose and close your eyes. Now visualize something nice and calming like sleeping in the middle of a forest or open field and staring at the clear sky. All your worries have left you and you are feeling extremely light and happy. This is the simplest form of meditation that there is, though be careful not to let anything distract those pleasant thoughts. If you do, start again and practice until the negative thoughts of the day and the interruptions stop. It takes practice but can be equated to something as simple as daydreaming.

Do this for about 15 minutes a day.

Benefits of this type of meditation:

The benefits are multiple. You can overcome stigmas, find yourself move past all of your self-esteem problems and this leads to a more peaceful existence with yourself. This means that mental strain is less and that you lead a more positive life. Positivity is very good for your health and, in turn, helps your immune system to stave off the effects of illnesses. If you imagine pleasant things and let them penetrate into your mind, you are letting go of negative things and this helps you to become much more positive in your approach to life.

MEDITATION

Vipasana meditation

This form of meditation practice is also known as mindfulness meditation. This type helps you in cleansing your respiratory tract and also helps you clear your mind.

How to perform:

To perform this type of an exercise, sit with legs folded.

Maintain a straight back and draw in a few deep breaths. Increase the intensity of your breath and start to draw the breath from your stomach. After a couple of minutes, increase the intensity of your exhale breath and reduce the time taken to inhale. This type of meditation is explained in more detail in the final chapter because it's more complex and can be performed even during your general day to day activities. Stop, take in the atmosphere and the ambiance and allow your thought processes to stop and to be bathed in the moment.

Repeat it for 15 minutes and you can perform this exercise once a day for not more than 15-20 minutes.

The benefits of this type of meditation

Mindfulness meditation makes you much more aware of your surroundings. It helps you to find a peaceful balance so that you can live your life in a more relaxed way. It is useful for those suffering from anxiety and also for those who want to feel better about being themselves. In the world of today, people are getting away from the basics of living their lives to the full. They forget the power of the mind, and the word "mindfulness" is a reminder of how powerful the mind can be. Be aware of it; allow your breathing to help you to avoid respiratory problems and also to make you feel very aware of yourself and your place within your surroundings. This will sharpen your thought processes and make you a much happier, more fulfilled person.

CHAPTER 5

Precautions to Observe

"Work is not always required. There is such a thing as sacred idleness"

George MacDonald

In the previous chapter, we looked at the various forms of meditation practices and how you can perform them to attain a sense of calm.

When all is said and done, you have to realize that too much of something can be a bad thing. And that rule applies to meditation as well. When you undertake meditation, you have to realize that it will have to be done within the right limits. You must also remember that you will have to keep in mind the various settings that will allow you to concentrate on your practice and help you add leverage to it.

Let us begin by looking at the right settings:

The right setting for meditation

Place

Before you sit down to meditate, you have to make sure that you find the right place. The place needs to be clean and there should be no clutter. Preferably somewhere that makes you feel naturally relaxed is good. Although it is advisable for you to sit directly on the floor, you can also sit on a chair or a stool if you have back or leg problems. Some people use a yoga mat or if they kneel, they use a cushion over their legs to protect the body from cramps and to stop circulation problems that may otherwise occur.

You must ideally have a clear view of nature in front of you when you sit down to meditate or at least have a poster of nature. You can also place a calming picture of the Buddha in front of you or have an object to focus on in the event that you choose to meditate with your eyes open. Some people do this and having something that gives you that extra focus is helpful.

You also need a place that is not too lit up. The dim light of early morning sun is ideal but if you choose a place indoors, then this should be somewhere where you can dim the light and feel safe and comfortable. Aromas are quite important. If you choose a place that is not too filled with aromas that are strong, this helps because it stops you from getting too distracted from what it is you are trying to achieve.

A room should also have windows that do not show busy streets outside, as these can prove to be distracting.

Position

When you sit down to meditate, you have to make sure that you assume the lotus pose or one of the variants shown on the page linked to in a previous chapter. The lotus pose is when where you sit with your legs folded and your hands stretched out. You have to place the back of your palms on your knees and join the tips of your index and thumb fingers. You must maintain a straight back and breathe in and out. You must also close your eyes and sit with a clear mind if your chosen style of meditation calls for this. Focused meditation is used when you find that you are able to concentrate on one focal spot rather than closing your eyes. Some people find this to be very beneficial.

Atmosphere

When you sit down to meditate, make sure that the atmosphere is calm and free from noise. If it is the natural sound of birds chirping then it is fine, but if it is the noise of traffic or some other such sound then it will disturb you and disrupt your practice. Turn off music, as this is a real distraction. Although music can be calming, it does tend to distract your mind from the purpose of your meditation moment.

Precautions

Physical implications

If you over-meditate then it can have a few physical implications.

To begin with, after you get up, you might not be able to feel your legs as a lot of lactic acid would have accumulated and they can go numb. If this is the case, then you do need to find a better position. Meditation is not about torture. It's about centralizing yourself and focusing upon what you are doing. The ideal position is, of course, the lotus position, though if you are new to meditation, instructors will be able to show you positions that are easier for you to achieve until you are more experienced.

Secondly, you will face temporary blindness after having your eyes closed for a long time. This is perfectly normal as it would be had you been in a dark room for any length of time. Before getting up and getting on with your day, calmly open your eyes and re-adjust to the ambient light. Then you will be able to adjust easily without endangering yourself.

Mental implications

Many times, after you finish meditating, you will feel like going back into a trance because it's a comfortable state to be in. You will be tempted to continue and go back to the subconscious state. It is better that you set yourself times for meditation and keep to them, since the benefits you have already gleaned from your session will help you to face the world as a stronger person.

You might also feel a little dizzy and find it difficult to walk in a straight line. You are therefore advised to sit with your eyes open for a few minutes and regain your full consciousness or awareness. This isn't really any different from waking up from a deep sleep and just as you would have to adjust to being awake, you need to adjust your mental state to this new sense of awakening.

These are just some of the side effects of meditation that you will have to be wary of and try and prevent difficulties arising from them, as much as is possible.

Overall help that your meditation sessions will give you

Provided that you are sensible in your approach to meditation, you will find that the benefits are fairly immediate. You may find it takes you a couple of sessions to feel more confident in your abilities to meditate. It is also likely that you will find that thoughts get in the way. This shouldn't put you off trying. It's a normal response. If you think that a healthy person can have hundreds of thoughts invading their minds within the time you took to meditate, it would actually be surprising if you were able to lock out all of those thoughts in the early stages of meditation.

When you are able to do that, you will feel fresher and sharper and the meditation skill is one of those skills where you instantly know you got something right. If you do think of things during the course of your meditation session that you should not be allowing to invade your thought processes, simply try to switch the distraction off and go back to concentrating on the system of meditation that you have chosen as one suitable for you. Never give up. It's a very worthwhile process and it takes time. Don't think of yourself as a failure. Think of yourself as being someone who is trying to improve life and who is experiencing difficulties. You can do it if you look at your mistakes and learn from them.

MEDITATION

Counting Breaths isn't Like Counting Sheep

"Just close your eyes and count your breaths," they say. How simple can it be? "Don't think about anything else though. Just concentrate on your breathing." Well, anyone who has tried this "simple" meditation knows that it just isn't that easy.

There are many obstacles to this seemingly effortless task. Our minds tend to wander naturally so if we try to completely focus on anything for more than a few seconds, random thoughts take over. Breathing is boring; let's face it. How can you concentrate on something so mundane when there are much more interesting things racing around in your head?

A typical session might go like this: I close my eyes, sit comfortably, and begin counting. Inhale one, inhale two, inhale... "Am I doing this right? I guess so, I'm already on... oh three." Inhale four... "Now, am I supposed to start over at one or just keep going?" Inhale one, inhale two, inhale three, and inhale four. "Wow, I'm really getting the hang of this. Oops." Inhale one, inhale two... "Did I remember to pay the phone bill? I'm sure I did. I'm really good at staying on top of my bills. I'm not like Susan, she's always... Darn, I did it again." Inhale one, inhale two...

The good news is, it does get better with practice. The bad news is, it can still be a struggle for experienced meditators, especially during busy or turbulent periods in their lives. Luckily, there is more good news. There are some specific things you can do to help you focus and reduce the frustration in your meditation practice. In this article, I would like to offer three tips to help you with your practice. They are: Observe don't control, be compassionate, and enjoy yourself.

First, don't force or try to control your breathing. This is a mistake that a lot of beginners make. Many inexperienced meditators consciously or unconsciously alter their breathing in an effort to focus on it. What it results is an exaggerated and often irregular breathing pattern. This can actually inhibit your meditation rather than help it.

What you want to do is just "watch" your breathing. You don't have to exert any additional effort at all. If you just wait and observe, you will breathe. Then, you can count. Of course, we all know this but many people still find themselves forcing it. If you catch yourself controlling your breaths, just gently remind yourself that it's not necessary and then wait for the next breath to come naturally.

This brings me to the next tip, which is compassion. In this case, I mean for you in your meditation practice. As we've been discussing, it's not an easy thing to do to concentrate on one's breath. It's very important not to scold yourself when your mind wanders or you catch yourself controlling your breathing. If you think about it, the time you would spend reprimanding yourself for breaking your focus is just more time away from your meditation. It is best to softly bring yourself back to your practice as soon as you notice you're wavering. Don't get down on yourself and start thinking, "I can't do this. This is never going to work for me." These negative thoughts do nothing to help your practice and waste valuable time. Be compassionate. Just brush it off and return to your meditation.

Another way to look at these wanderings is to realize that they are an important part of your progression. Meditation is a skill. And like most skills, it requires practice. A baseball player doesn't step into the batter's box for the first time and start hitting homeruns. He makes mistakes and corrections, and then improves over time. He can then gauge his progress by the reduction of errors. Even after he is an experienced batsman, he will still strike out more often than he would like. But his hits should increase as well.

In your meditation practice, your mind will likely wander more in the beginning. But don't give up. It will get better. Just like the baseball player, you will realize fewer mistakes over time and you will learn to recover from them more quickly. Sure, you will still have challenges and even slumps from time to time but you will also have more successes.

The final tip I would like to offer, is to find enjoyment in your practice. Even though it may be tough at times, daily meditation can greatly enhance your life. Don't rate yourself and expect to progress or improve to a particular degree within a particular timeframe. Unlike baseball, mediation is a life-long experience. Remember this is your time. Let it be your oasis, not a chore. No matter what else is going on in your life, your meditation time can be your escape. As a Zen master once said, "It's just you and your breath and then it's just your breath." Breathe in, breathe out, and forget about the world around you. Even when you're busy or preoccupied with some problem, even if you can only find ten or fifteen minutes to be alone with your breath, enjoy it.

I hope these tips will help you to enhance your meditation experience. They have certainly proved to be valuable in my own practice over the years. Of course I still struggle from time to time with the very same issues we've discussed here. But through observing rather than controlling, being compassionate to myself when I falter, and enjoying my special time alone; I have made my life fuller and happier.

Meditation for People on the Go

Meditation is an ancient ritual that's perfect for individuals seeking a bit of peace, quiet, and inner reflection into their daily lives. However, many individuals erroneously believe they don't have the appropriate time to devote to meditation. This practice does not require a special room and hours upon hours of inner reflection to be done properly and receive the best results. In fact, meditation can be done in any quiet corner, including your living room, office, or hotel.

In order to achieve the proper meditation in some of these places, you may need to practice certain techniques or bring along special devices that will block noise and ensure silence for your designated meditation time.

MEDITATION

Consider joining a meditation group so that you can effectively learn the methods of meditation before you attempt to meditate in unusual surroundings. The techniques and methods you learn through a meditation instructor will help you accomplish your own personal goals of meditation and inner exploration.

Meditation does not have to be incredibly time consuming. Make it a point to dedicate a few minutes each day to your meditation goals and spend some time reflecting inward. Mornings are excellent times to begin meditation since you are the most at ease during this time and your home is probably the quietest. Consider waking up before the rest of your household to snag a few much needed minutes along in order to successfully complete your meditation process. This is critical for both men and women with children who find it hard to meditate amidst the noises and demands of children.

When you are on the go, do not leave your meditation practices at home! Consider snatching up a pair of noise canceling headphones to block out noise on trains, planes, or automobiles. This will allow you the greatest sense of peace and quiet so that you can continue with your meditation techniques. Bring along a special meditation soundtrack, or familiar tunes to which you can also block out unnecessary background noise in order to meditate.

Meditation can be an excellent way to unwind after a long day of traveling, so consider taking time to practice your techniques once you reach your destination. For individuals who are constantly calling hotel rooms home, it can be quite easy to miss your personal meditation space. For this reason, carry a small token or a few items with you on your travels to remind you of home. Consider bringing a favorite blanket, pillow, or mat to aid you in your meditation practices. Also, bring along a photograph of your family or friends to help with the homesickness.

Use scents to transport you to a more serene world. Aromatherapy has been used in conjunction with meditation for thousands of years.

MEDITATION

Consider beginning your meditation to comforting or exotic smells of incense and candles. For individuals on the go, consider bringing along travel candles or a vial of essential oil that you can leave open to pervade the atmosphere.

CHAPTER 6

Expectations and Exercises

"The way to do, is to be."

Lao Tzu

When you start with the process of meditation, you have to understand that you need to have reasonable expectations. If you do not, then you set yourself up for disappointment and that goes against the whole process of what meditation is all about.

You cannot expect too much and then wonder what went wrong. You will be disappointed if you want too much out of it and not be able to fulfill all your expectations straight away. It takes years of practice before you become a master and even masters are improving their techniques all of the time. Never take for granted that you will perfect the art of meditation since there is always room for improvement.

You must understand that meditation is a mere tool for you to remedy your stress and not a cure. It is just a form of treatment that will help reduce your worries and shrink your problems. You have the power within your mind to do all of that, but since you have lived your life for a period of time, you have to be aware that you have also built up habits in your behavior that you need to overcome in order to meditate successfully. The more time you give the learning process, the better you will become at it and the more your body will benefit from what meditation is doing. Remember, in a previous chapter, we linked to proof that meditation can actually make you feel younger. It took you a while to reach the age that you are, so give it time to work its wonders on you, and don't expect instant results. Some people do achieve a sense of well being early on in their experience, while others need more time.

Unlike drugs and alcohol, which will act as mere band aids and help cover the wound for some time and then push you back into your old life, meditation will help in reducing your problems and not merely masking them. That's a very valuable asset to have on your side.

It will alter your thought process and help in generating endorphins. These endorphins will keep you happy and stress free and the more you meditate the more that these endorphins get released.

It is therefore important to meditate on a very regular basis and not simply use it as a tool during times of stress.

The body will not accept the practice if you take breaks from meditating or perform it randomly. You have to establish a routine and make meditating a habit.

And once it turns into a habit, your mind will not have to put in too much effort to constantly tell you to start meditating. You have to start putting your mind on autopilot and sit down to meditate.

You must also remember to meditate at the same time daily so that your body will get used to it. You must start by warming up no matter how far you are into your practice. By warming up, you will not just add leverage to your practice but also develop the patience to sit through it.

Warming up exercises for meditation

The whole idea of limbering up exercises before meditation sessions is to help the body adjust to the new relaxed position. These are very easy to do. If you are simply having a short mindfulness meditation session, then these are not so necessary because this form of meditation can be done in a short space of time. Thus, exercising would extend that time too much and make the shorter session that you require amid your busy day too onerous.

However, if you want to make the most out of your meditation, these help you because they tense the body and then relax it which sets the mood for perfect meditation practice.

Hands against head

Clasp the cup of your hands against your forehead and press. This must be done with a little pressure and with your hand curled up. Hold for a few moments. Then move your hands flat against your face, which is of course much more relaxed. Leave the hands there for a moment.

The second exercise also involves the fists. Hold your hands out in front of you and make a tight fist. Then slacken the fist and hold your hand out as if receiving something. This helps to make the hands much more relaxed and helps relieve anger.

Arms

In this exercise, hold one arm out to the side, parallel with your shoulder. Move the other arm over so that it crosses your chest and your hand touches the arm just above the armpit area. Now reverse this and do it with the other arm.

Place your fists onto your neck at each side of the head. Rotate the arm from the elbow forward five times and back five times. This helps flexibility. Another exercise you can use is to hold your arm out in front of you and then clasp your other arm, both hands holding onto the opposite arm just above wrist level. Circle the arms bringing them up together toward your body and circling them away from your body and back again. This is useful to get rid of any muscular knots.

A head and neck exercise

This is particularly useful if you have a lot on your mind and are not yet ready to go into your meditation state. This helps to relieve the muscles around the neck area that is particularly prone to aches caused by stress. Look to the right, moving your head so that it looks over your right shoulder, and then move it to the left doing the same thing. Move the head so you are looking upward and then downward. These are slow movements that enable you to feel the muscles in the neck loosen up. These should be performed about 5 times for each side and once for up and down.

Body exercises

These are performed to give your body more suppleness. Stand with your legs a little apart and without taking your feet from the floor twist your body around to the right from the waist area. Then back to a central position and finally twist the other way. Repeat these exercises up to ten times. These help to loosen the knot in your stomach area and give the body more flexibility.

Stretching exercises

These are particularly beneficial before a meditation session. Stretch your hands above your head, lean over to the right and then to the left. Leg stretching is particularly relevant, as this will help you to hold the meditation poses that may help your experience. For the leg stretches, you need to keep your feet together and stand upright. Then bend so that you are touching your toes. Pull your rear end outward and lower yourself until you find that you are in a crouched position and then gradually stand up again until you are once again touching your toes.

These may sound rather a lot of exercises, though they are very simple to perform and there are more exercises if you should need them, which merely stretch the area of, the body where you find is most stressed. For example, stretch skyward with your arms, if you have heavy shoulders and then circle the arms. If your neck hurts, lean forward as far as you can, stretching the tendons at the back of the neck by tucking your chin into your chest. Then slowly raise the head until you are looking up as far as you can. Repeat these exercises several times until you feel the benefit of the exercise and are sufficiently relaxed to meditate.

CHAPTER 7

What Professional Doctors Say About Meditation

"To understand the immeasurable, the mind must be extraordinarily quiet, still."

Jiddu Krishnamurti

It's vital that you take in what professionals say about the benefits of meditation. These are people that you entrust your health to and if you know that you have the backing of the medical field, then this may give you more confidence to carry on with your meditation practice on a regular basis.

In a report by Robert Puff, Ph.D, a study done by Harvard Medical School and the Beth Israel Deaconess Medical center shows that more doctors are actually prescribing meditation for patients on a regular basis. When you think of the benefits these are so many that it makes sense that they do continue to prescribe this form of therapy for their patients. Without the use of medications, these treatments work out relatively cheap in comparison with traditional therapies and can actually help you to get into good habits that in turn make you feel fitter and more mentally agile than before.

This has to say something about the benefits derived from meditation and the way in which the mind can be assisted in its management of stress in day to day life. If this can also help in diminishing the amount of anti-depressants being prescribed, this means that people are finding their way using natural methods, rather than depending upon drugs to do the work for them. This can be extremely useful and mean that people are able to get back to being productive much earlier than they would be on prescribed medications.

Scientific American ran a report that showed moderate proof that meditation helps with depression and anxiety and also with pain management. The report, issued in May 2014, reported a study on a small group of individuals with similar symptoms and background to see if those who practiced meditation did better than those who did not. The positivity of this report was indicative that meditation does help, though the scientists wanted to keep an open mind because they thought that meditation should be given larger trials before conclusive evidence could be confirmed. However, there are two ways of looking at this report. Those seeking help from meditation may be pulled toward the positive aspects that the report did not write off the benefits of meditation, while skeptics may want to wait until more evidence is available from a scientific viewpoint.

One study that was rather interesting was done on African Americans and showed a distinct advantage to those who underwent transcendental meditation, in that they tested African American women and men with cardiovascular diseases. The conclusions were startling in that they confirmed that this kind of meditation could actually prevent myocardial infarction and stroke in those participants who were using the meditation system to support their health. This is a very great breakthrough for those with heart problems, since many will die or suffer incapacitating illness because of their heart problems under normal treatment circumstances. The study done by The Institution for Natural Medicine and Prevention was amazing and gave hope to many that their condition could be controlled to such an extent by the use of meditation that it meant the difference between life and death.

A further study done by the Institute of Psychological Research in conjunction with Leiden University in Holland found that meditation actually triggered the parts of the brain which are responsible for creativity and that people who performed meditation on a regular basis were more likely to be creative and be able to think "outside of the box" and use their creativity productively. This isn't surprising since meditation stops the flow of life sufficiently to allow a person to let their creative sidekick in. If you are busy, for example, with a pressured life, you don't give yourself the time for that part of the brain responsible for creativity to actually do anything. With meditation, the study showed that those who did perform meditation on a regular basis were helping both convergent and divergent thought processes, which makes them more open to creativity.

There is so much evidence out there on the benefits of meditation that one cannot help but be pulled into the truth of how meditation helps the body. UCLA researchers came up with something even more startling, in that they found that the formation of the brain itself in those who meditate on a regular basis was different, and that folds had appeared in the cerebral cortex. What this meant was that the brain was able to process information in a faster and more efficient way, thus favoring meditation as opening up the ability to learn faster and to have a sharper learning curve.

Meditation has many benefits. Those who practice it swear by its efficiency, though when you look at the number of aspects that meditation touches upon, it's small wonder that the medical world is trying its best to decide whether to discredit it in favor of standard medications or to favor it on the basis that it is a natural way for people to manage their illnesses, their potential for illnesses and their own levels of anxiety without the use of expensive medications that require long term commitment.

When you look at the amount of money spent in the United States on anti-depressants in one year, it's horrific. The rise in use by teens as far back as 2011 was 400 percent, and that figure continues to rise. With teens attending classes for meditation, they could be helped before anxiety sets in and find themselves more grounded and able to take on the stresses of the world without such medications. Similarly, women who were taking medications such as Effexor, Celexa, Zoloft etc., increased in number so that in 2011 there was shown to be 23 per cent of all women between the ages of 40 and 50. These numbers continue to rise and are a worrying reflection of the kind of world that we are living in today. Those in this age group are in the later years of their careers and have potentially had to deal with progress and the changes that go with it. The unacceptably high proportion of women taking medication for depression or depression related illnesses could be refocused on natural treatments such as meditation in order to help the patients gain control of their lives.

Unfortunately, once a patient is on these kinds of drugs, they are usually on them long term because these are not drugs that you can simply stop taking. While some may see it as a "conspiracy" theory, with all of the supported evidence shown above, can one not be a little suspect about the profits of pharmaceutical companies weighed up against the promotion of natural health cures that cost nothing at all?

The medical world is mostly in agreement about the benefits of meditation. They see this as a breakthrough. People themselves are finding that meditation is benefiting them. There are many reports on this and videos on websites such as YouTube, which show the benefits of meditation, and yet people still resist it. The problem is that people find it hard to go backward and they find getting off the roundabout of activity and stress very hard indeed, although once they do, they wish they had done it earlier, because it allows them such freedom.

Talk to your doctor. Talk to yoga practitioners and even if you take up yoga as something you think you can do, through this medium you will be introduced to meditation and can then expand your view of meditation based upon your yoga experience. For most people, yoga sessions are available locally and this is a step toward actually incorporating meditation into your life. This first step in the right direction could benefit your body, your mind and your ability to stave off the effects of anxiety. If you talk to your practicing general practitioner about meditation, she/ he may be a little wary. Try talking to them about yoga, and as this is an established beneficial activity, they are more likely to say that this will benefit the health. What they are failing to see is that yoga in itself introduces practitioners to meditation and that meditation may be what is helping the body and mind to stay fit.

The Buddha used meditation to get clarity so that he would be able to explain to those wishing to follow Buddhist ways of life how they should behave toward others and toward themselves. There is very powerful evidence that Buddhism and the meditation that goes with it helps people to find a happier place within themselves where acceptance is easier than it would be without this discipline. People are able to find a complete peace within themselves using meditation of this kind and when you see conversations with powerful people such as the Dalai Lama, you cannot help but be impressed by his state of calm and it is this state of calm that people who are suffering from stress and anxiety seek. Of course, you don't have to shave your head or even don the robes of a Buddhist monk, but you do have to put aside time to allow yourself that silence that is as powerful as a healing tool.

Guided Meditation

There are many different methods of guided meditation. Since each person has a different goal when starting the meditation process, there are several ways to achieve these goals with diverse guided meditation programs. There are a few steps that the meditating person must go through in order to achieve a complete meditative state. Most of these steps in the process focus mainly on relaxation and the clearing of the mind since it can be a difficult task to achieve.

People who find interest in meditation turn to guided meditation to help them to center their minds and bodies. The guided meditation process can make meditating seem achievable and can help the user to feel more grounded and in touch with themselves rather than feeling lost while trying to quiet their mind.

There are many different ways to achieve a meditative state but most of these processes start by instructing the person to sit in a comfortable position. It is also very important that the person is in a quiet space with no distractions or sounds around that could divert the concentration that is needed. Guided meditation generally instructs the person who is meditating to quiet and stop the mind. This means that the person should release any thoughts from his or her mind and concentrate on nothingness. The meditating person should also make sure that his or her body is completely relaxed and there is no strain on any body part while sitting in the position.

Meditation chairs can upgrade the experience of investigation by permitting you to sit in a comfortable and loose position amid your relaxing session. On the off chance that you have back issues or constrained adaptability, the seat offers a comfortable option for sitting on the floor.

For those simply who are starting the meditation, a sitting chair can be a successful method for upgrading focus and concentration. There are distinctive sorts of seats accessible including meditation seats, ergonomically designed tilt chairs and inflatable cushions.

A meditation chair allows you to sit comfortably without putting pressure on your back. A tilt chair can also support your back and this is will be allowing you to remain in the perfect upright position. A lot of companies that provides meditation supplies also manufacture sell some meditation chairs, inflatable cushions and folding benches, to enable you to meditate in any setting or environment. A perfect chair is an excellent investment if you are continuously exercising meditation.

Meditation chairs have many types of advantages more than just sitting on the floor or a regular chair. Meditation needs harmony of body and mind, which means that physical discomfort should not really exist during the meditation experience. To expand our consciousness and reach clarity of mind, it is really important to be as comfortable as you can get during the meditation session. Sitting in any position for a long time is bound to cause cramping and distress. The designed chairs can provide the proper support and comfort necessary to allow you to get all what you need of your meditation experience. It is also very important to know that regular chairs do not mold to the body in the same way as an ergonomically designed meditation device.

The perfect meditation chairs have a slight forward angle, which prevents you from slumping during the meditation session. However, make sure that the chair is not too steeply angled, as this might cause overarching. The ideal tilt should be no more than a few inches. The most effective option is to purchase a meditation chair that you are capable of adjusting according to your height, weight and comfort level. Having an experienced person who is there to guide you through the meditation session and adjust your posture is also a great idea.

A sitting device may be in so many ways useful if you are practicing Zen meditation, which needs many sitting postures. Zen meditation chairs can be made out of a lot of materials and come in several different styles. You can pick up c the style that suits you the best as long as the device enables your diaphragm to contract and expand in a free way.

Meditation is all about discovering your inner peace. As opposed to prevalent thinking, discipline and physical uneasiness degrades instead of improving the experience. A meditation chair is a device that helps us to focus on the most important thing during our meditation session. With the proper tools and surroundings, the meditation session will surely be the best experience you ever had.

CHAPTER 8

Meditation – Focused Meditation Versus Mindfulness

For people who do not really understand much about meditation, an argument may come to mind as to whether you can be mindful as well as meditating. People see meditation as a closing of the mind or a switching off of activities within the brain with focus being on chant, mantras, focused objects or breathing sounds. How does this then equate with mindfulness?

If you are mindful doesn't that make you very conscious and very aware?

The truth is that there are different ways to meditate. Some do focus on inner elements such as the heartbeat or the breathing, but these are all very positive things. Even with mindful meditation, it helps to be aware of the breathing because people have learned so many bad habits that this takes away the benefit of good oxygenation to the body. However, mindful meditation goes a little further than other forms of meditation, in that you don't have to sit cross legged all of the time you are meditating. People who have mastered this kind of meditation find themselves present in the actual moment and are aware of their surroundings and things that people have long forgotten about as important.

The mindfulness doesn't mean filling the mind with worries and anxieties. It means dropping those in favor of being totally aware of the moment. That may sound a little wishy-washy for people who are new to meditation, so let's explain it another way. Instead of the stress of a moment, someone who practices mindfulness allows the positivity within their surroundings to penetrate into their minds, leaving no space for negativity.

If you stand in a garden and look at the cobwebs that are forming on the plants, these may be filled with morning dew. The sparkle of the cobweb will give the impression of becoming a diamond necklace. It's a beautiful sight to behold. Those too busy with life would pass by it and not see it for what it is. Those who are mindful of that moment would embrace the experience as being something that is filled with wonderment.

Being mindful does not mean that you cannot meditate because your mind is too busy. The kind of mindfulness that you practice is concentrating on one moment in your life and that's a help, in itself. If you concentrate on one moment, for example, you are unable to allow other thoughts that are negative from the past to interfere, and you are also unable to plan in advance and have your mind filled with ambitious thoughts. Being planted in the moment makes you much more aware of everything around you and able to take things in your pace. This cuts down on stress levels. It helps people to be able to go through their lives and to practice meditation at any time they wish.

Transcendental meditation calls for silence of the mind. Focused attention meditation uses an object as a focal point and exercises the front area of the brain, helping those who use this form of meditation to gain focus within their lives.

Mindfulness takes all of the actual process of evaluation and manipulation out of the picture and teaches practitioners to accept that which is presented without question and without any kind of mental fight. This allows alpha brain waves to fill the mind and it is these that give the subject such a feeling of well-being and relaxation. Thus, the subject is not actively thinking of anything and one could describe their mind as empty as is the purpose in other forms of meditation, while mindful of its surrounding. It lets the surroundings permeate without having to actually give them sense or meaning.

This is extremely good for stressed people to practice and those who achieve it feel a certain sense of innocence. If you can imagine a baby lying in a cradle and looking up toward a bubble. It has no preconceived ideas about what the bubble is, nor whether it is solid or not. The baby sees it and accepts it for what it is. This simplicity of nature of acceptance is what mindfulness is all about – seeing, being mindful and accepting? Thus, although the mind is not empty of vision, it is empty of preconceived ideas about what the vision is showing it.

From this illustration, you should be able to see the difference between mindfulness meditation and other forms of meditation. The Buddha actually made the point of explaining to those seeking his help that the less you are, the more you are and this has been translated in many ways since. Mindfulness means awareness. It doesn't mean any action needs to be taken or any judgment made. Just like the innocent baby who saw the bubble, the mind sees the beauty of the earth and all that is in it and lets those visions permeate without having to have any interaction with them.

Finishing this chapter with a quotation about mindfulness, taken from "The Miracle of Mindfulness: An Introduction to the Practice of Meditation" seems very appropriate as giving the reader food for thought in their journey into the unknown world of meditation.

"Feelings, whether of compassion or irritation, should be welcomed, recognized, and treated on an absolutely equal basis; because both are ourselves. The tangerine I am eating is me. The mustard greens I am planting are me. I plant with all my heart and mind. I clean this teapot with the kind of attention I would have were I giving the baby Buddha or Jesus a bath. Nothing should be treated more carefully than anything else. In mindfulness, compassion, irritation, mustard green plant, and teapot are all sacred."

MEDITATION

Thích Nhất Hạnh

You have but one life. Mindfulness allows you maximum enjoyment and enlightenment from that moment you start to practice it as well as helping you to reap the mental and health benefits that come as part and parcel of your acceptance of this great form of relaxation and acceptance of life, as the gift it is.

CHAPTER 9

Creating Your Own Meditation Room

A lot of people are taking up the activity of yoga these days to keep themselves in peak health and far away from the dangers the stress of today's modern society can bring to a person. Yoga is a kind form of exercise, more kind than most of the other forms of exercise such as aerobics, weight lifting, or even something as simple as running! Most people who practice yoga have their very own private meditation rooms.

Meditation rooms don't have to be exactly rooms per se. Most of the time they're just secluded nooks and cranny's in someone's home where they can be in total isolation to be able to think, relax, and meditate. Having a private meditation room, however, is not something that has to be exclusive to yoga practitioners. You too can have your very own meditation room that can be used as a place to just sit back and get away from the fast-paced and stressful daily life that most of us live. Your meditation room can be your own hideaway, where you can breathe freely and gather your thoughts.

Choosing a Spot for Your Meditation Room

Silence and isolation are the primary qualities that a meditation room must have. No matter how small your home is, it is possible to have a meditation room where you can have a bit of peaceful respite. Just find a place to set it up that is a little out of the way in your home. You can situate your own meditation room in your own bedroom if need be. Any corner that can be made secluded will suffice, in fact. All you need to do if your meditation room is not a separate room in itself is to partition it creatively so you would not be bothered if you're inside your nook.

Furnishing the Meditation Room

A meditation room doesn't require much in terms of furnishing. The most essential piece of furniture there is, would be a comfortable chair that is wide enough for you to curl your legs in. Even that, a chair is not exactly necessary. If space is a problem, a cushion can serve in its stead.

A CD player, however, may be necessary. It helps a lot to meditate while listening to soft, instrumental music. Or perhaps to recorded natural sounds like the singing of the birds, the sound of the waves, and the sound of falling rain.

How your meditation room is lit may affect how well you focus and concentrate in clearing your mind. The lighting you ought to install in your meditation room is something that should be soft and subtle. Stay away from harshly glowing fluorescent bulbs when you're lighting your meditation room.

You do not have to decorate the walls of your meditation room. If you can paint the walls a neutral color, it would be best to do so. You don't need anything that can distract you from meditation inside your meditation room. To set and enhance the mood, however, you can put shelves where you can place some scented candles or a vase of flowers, perhaps even a figurine or two. A potted plant can help set the mood as well. These are all the decorations you would need for your meditation room.

Maintaining the Meditation Room

Your meditation room is ideally the one place in your house, if not in the whole world, where you can get away to relax and to clear your mind of anything that is bothering you. The one thing that will defeat this purpose is if you leave your meditation room cluttered.

No matter how busy you may be with your daily life, always find the time to keep your meditation room clean and free of clutter. Cleaning your meditation room may be seen as a form of meditation in itself. After all, the reason you have a meditation room is to keep your mind clear and unburned by chaos. To achieve that, you have to keep your meditation room clean and unburned by chaos as well.

You Do Not Need a Meditation Room

Even though we have covered the concept of meditation rooms does not mean that you need one. All you really need is a relaxing corner in order to perform meditation. If this is the corner of your living room, then that is enough to suffice for you. You do not need anything special to meditate. All you really need is a clear space and a clear mind in order to perform this exercise. That is one of the best parts of meditation ... no equipment needed.

CHAPTER 10

Positive Affirmation in Meditation

As a human being it is very important and extremely crucial to have a positive self-esteem for our well being and happiness. Our self-esteem being positive is what makes the difference as to what we take on in life and how we decide to create and what we push to achieve. In order for us to have a happy and healthy relationship with other people along with experiencing intimacy that is really true we must have a positive self-esteem. You could also think of having a positive self-esteem can grant us a pure spirituality. A poor self-esteem can allow us to be pulled down to a large amount of negativity in our life. These include anxiety, depression, stress, fear and loneliness. Having a poor self-esteem or negative attitude is believed to correspond with a drug or alcohol dependency. There are some people who believe that a self-image that is poor or negative can be the reason for these addictions.

When we look at self-esteem and its importance we think we can understand it somewhat, but there is always the question that has remained unanswered about how we can enhance or improve some ones self-esteem. There are some who believe that self-esteem is controlled by a person being successful, by accomplishing the tasks that they take on during their lifetime. Because of this a lot of effort is place on assisting other people in efficiently and effectively planning what they will do in life. Some think that our relationships are what determine our self-esteem, or that if we are surrounded by positive people who acknowledge or appreciate us that it will affect our self-esteem in a positive manner. There is training that can be given to help improve a person's interpersonal skills such as relating and communicating with other people. Positive self-esteem is not gained by doing or having these skills even though they both are still very important.

MEDITATION

Positive affirmations are an extremely effective way to help improve one's self-esteem. A person will ultimately change how they act towards others or how they see them or even what they think about themselves through positive affirmations. Our positive affirmations help us decide what decisions we are going to make from what we feel inside our mind. The attitude or personality, our identities of who we see ourselves as, our way of thinking all come from the affirmations that we have. These are fundamentally composed of mere language or words. All the thoughts and all the ways we think are our affirmations. When we use affirmations that are positive repetitively we will change the internal prevalent language pattern. Although it sounds like a bad thing we are capable of having negative affirmations that we can use constant positive affirmations to change the way we think giving us internal positive dialogue or self-talk.

Using our own voice can be the best way to use our positive affirmations. We can listen to a product that is developed for commercial use and gain beneficial results from the positive affirmations found within. You can help to improve the power of these commercial products by using your own voice to quote them. This makes it easier because the resistance is much less when the voice your mind hears is already a familiar voice and it hears it all day. Now apply the positive affirmation.

Music that is for therapeutic relaxation can help to strengthen the positive affirmations alongside using your own voice. Using your own voice for your positive affirmations can be extremely powerful and therapeutic relaxation music that will help to create an audio space making the affirmations when we are relaxed it is possible to be more suggestible or open to positive affirmations. Therapeutic relaxation music can be enhanced greatly by combining it with binaural audio tones and the delivery of positive enhancing affirmations that will have a high amount of effect on improving and transforming someone's internal self-esteem and self-talk. Using affirmations that are recorded in someone's own voice and using therapeutic relaxation type music of the most common methods of treatment for someone who is suffering from substance abuse problems. It is a great method of improving someone's self-esteem that is a great method of utilizing affirmations.

Law of Attraction: How to Use Affirmations

In order to affirm something means to declare that something is true and already existent. It works the same when you want to attract things or transform something into one of our desires. In order to create an affirmation, one must declare to the universe and to yourself that you already are what you want to be. As you repeat the affirmations you must hold your thoughts clear and use intense focus on what you intend to create. This is what makes the time that you are meditating perfect for repeating affirmations.

Affirmations serve a lot of different purposes when you are trying to manifest what you want out of life. Applying the laws of attraction can be extremely hard while you are trying to maintain a positive and uplifting thought process. For most people, it is very difficult to monitor every thought that goes through your head. However, once you create very clear affirmations, you can use them to control your thoughts and influence your thought process toward a more positive thought process in general.

Three Ways to Use Affirmations

1. One of the first steps to using affirmations is to explain very clear about what you want from the universe. In order to become clear enough for the universe to recognize your affirmations, you should write out in full details what you want to experience and see in your goal. The clearer you are about your intentions to change things and what you want to manifest, the more power you have to create what you really want.

2. Write your positive affirmation in the first person stating, what you want from life the easier it is to manifest. Do not state that you "wish" or "someday." You should completely omit the

words "I wish," "someday" or "I don't want to."

When considering affirmations, you should make "I am" statements.

3. Always make sure that you enter your affirmation zone with a positive feeling. You should always use your affirmation with a feeling that will empower your desires. These feelings generate the internal energy necessary to manifest what you want from the universe.

At times, people find it hard to create success with affirmations. This is because the energy we release into the universe has a lot to do with what we get back from the universe. In order to manifest positive things from the universe you must have a positive attitude. The affirmation must be more than just mindless, feeling-less repetition.

The Law of Attraction Can Help With Your Anxiety

The law of attraction has helped countless people, all over the world to develop ease over your stress and anxiety. If you are one of the tens of thousands of people who suffer from anxiety or high stress you will appreciate the fact that positive affirmations can help you to develop control over your anxiety and stress. You are not alone and the number of people who are suffering from anxiety and stress is rising daily. If you find that you are suffering from anxiety or stress you may need to seek the help of a licensed therapist.

While you are seeking the help of a licensed professional, you can use the laws of attraction to help speed up your recovery and aid the medication in treating your disorder. For many people who practice the law of attraction, it is the focal point of recovery. Licensed therapists recommend the practice because it dates back to the Ancient Babylonians because of its power to heal physical mental and emotional problems.

MEDITATION

Even though the practice is considered ancient and is well known to help people manifest things in their lives that they feel are important, the law of attraction has only recently made books for its ability to make lives better. It has mostly been passed down through word of mouth for those who practiced meditation or martial arts.

It is sad to think that we are just now learning how to take control of our own lives and we are just now learning that we are the creator of our own life experience. Whether we are religious or not, we now recognize that some supernatural being is not in charge our lives. While there may be a higher power, we are in the driver's seat of our lives and we choose which roads we want to take and what turns we want to take in life. These turns can lead us to success or can lead us to falling flat on our face.

The best part is that we don't have to wait for things to come to us in life, we can start today and create a life that we feel is worth living.

Three Simple Steps to Enhance Your Therapy

1. Did you know that meditating for at least 10 -20 minutes every day on a regular basis, will help you greatly to improve your condition? But you still might need the help of a professional therapist or doctor but practicing meditation everyday yourself is still a valuable thing. On the off chance that you have youngsters or other relatives that need your consideration you need to do this activity when things are peaceful with the goal that you can really be still and relaxed. Create some time for mediation from a busy and stressful day.

2. At the point when thinking you can do the meditation session: Close your eyes and imagine yourself sitting in a huge football stadium all by yourself in total darkness. Hold this mental picture for around 20 seconds. After the 20 seconds are over envision yourself sitting in the same stadium with bright and warm lights sparkling on you, after that do a reversal in your mind to the same stadium with each one of

the lights out. This exercise is going to enhance the understanding of your inner self. To know your inner person meditation will help you to understand yourself. It will likewise help you to hear yourself out and turn out tó be more natural. The Law of Attraction has helped endless individuals to help with their tensions and anxiety. It might be troublesome at first for you to have a meditation session particularly on the off chance that you didn't do meditation even before. You still want to make it part of your daily routine. Meditation is really helpful for good mental and physical health.

3. To help with your stress you can likewise consider some awesome affirmations to assist you those lines of recovery. Here are a few sentences of what you could say while doing affirmations: "I am living in heaven and I have peace all around me. I am feeling extraordinary and I cherish my life". You will have to say these affirmations in the present tense. This may sound like a lie to you at first, when you are feeling quiet to the contrary. The Law of Attraction helps us to understand that the universe however will only respond to your feelings not to the spoken language. Affirmations are totally going to help you to train your subconscious mind to be in harmony with the way of exactly how you want it to be. When using the Law of Attraction to become well and to get rid of stress both meditation and affirmations are important. This will be an amazing steppingstone into your future free from stress and anxieties.

With the information about the Law of Attraction and by applying it in the right way we can program ourselves to be what we truly need to be. We really don't need to think that our conditions in life are meant to be or that we having to depend on external forces and their mercy! It is your right to have peace and good health when applying the Law of Attraction and when making it all work for you.

Self-Improvement with Affirmations

Did you know that affirmations are very powerful as tools that could be the key in bringing a whole new change in your life?

MEDITATION

Affirmations could bring you a change in your life or it could bring you new situations into your life. Self-affirmations are healing, optimistic messages that you can give to yourself to get rid of your negative messages. Affirmations are an example of visualization with mental images but in affirmations we use words instead. Words you say so everyone can hear, read or compose every day that will help you describe what you need to be and what you plan to accomplish.

Affirmations are self-improvement predictions that when imagined and had confidence in will work out as expected.

Just saying the words over and over again is not really enough. Affirmations are not some type of magic sentences that are said only a couple of times and after that makes miracles. If you want affirmations to produce results, they ought to be repeated frequently with feeling and conviction, in order for it to work.

In order to start successful affirmations you have to start by saying these words: "I am", "I can", and "I will". An "I am" affirmation is an announcement of who you are, for example, I am smart or I am creative. An "I can" affirmation is an announcement of your potential and power of changing, for example, I can be powerful or I can be a winner. An "I will" affirmation is an announcement of positive change that you need to fulfill, for example, I will remain calm or I will handle money related issues carefully today. Affirmations ought to dependably be expressed in a positive way. An incredible approach to use affirmations is to directly write down 30 of them, each on a different car. Every day of the month concentrate on one affirmation. Keep the card with you showed in your sight and read it out loud amid the day.

Affirmations are a very easy way for you to improve yourself because by nature humans are compelled to follow what they believe in. What keeps you moving is your belief in the final result. If you keep telling yourself something, your inner self will make it become true. Affirmations are capable of strengthen your ambition, create new solutions and activate the subconscious mind in order to make your affirmation come true. The affirmations that you keep repeating everyday will become a positive habit that will result in self-improvement of your mind, body and soul.

Positive Affirmations for the Sake of Meditation

There are positive affirmations that have been specially written to build up your meditation attitude and help you master the skills required to navigate this tricky discipline.

One of the basics of meditation is to be in a casual, cool, and even tranquil condition of being. And the perfect way to achieve this is to let go of all your worries, release stress, and let your internal thoughts become quiet mode. Our affirmations that were mentioned above are going to help you with all of this and a lot more, including focus, concentration, and even dedication to your practice of meditation.

You are able to use affirmations right before a meditation session to help settle your mind and prepare for your session to begin, or you can even choose one or two affirmations to focus on (or anchor) as a point during the meditation itself. Whichever you choose, we think you'll be amazed by the results it ends up with. We hope that our book will help you to meditate deeply and give you the peace you need and look for.

Meditation just acknowledges the past and in that way discharges itself from its talons. Whatever has happened they are just thoughts and they don't control us. They are basically discharged if they are destructive and celebrated if positive. It does not usually attempt to reprogram the past thought patterns or behaviors rather through the infusion of love in the mediator, it is felt that new, higher thought patterns naturally develop and old habits are released or transformed.

Affirmations can be a type of self-hypnosis where a word or an expression is repeated again and again as a method for reprogramming our subconscious. They are the most powerful affirmations when one is focused and concentrated but are effective even amidst the hustle and bustle of stress and tensions.

I have seen samples where individuals have perceived impulsive dietary patterns as a method for hiding oneself or subconsciously taking oneself out of the dating diversion in order to be free from being harmed seeing someone, On the other hand of smoking or medication addictions as a method of oneself over some form of guilt or self-hate. There are a lot of scenarios where, unless we explore our subconscious, we keep following and stressing ourselves with these extremely negative behaviors.

In my perspective, meditation is the least complex and best strategy for spiritual development. Unlike when we are doing prayers, where we lay out what we believe we need and do all the talking, meditation hands over the process to our heart and soul, or in some cases to God, and tells you directly do the talking and I will listen

Positive affirmations are something that you use to tell the universe what WILL be, not what you want. You will be successful, you will be positive, you will be exactly what you want to be in life and nothing can stand in your way.

In meditation the attention is on the heart and the spirit and the present minute. We leave the past and future and put the greater part of our consideration on 'now'. In the "now" in meditation we feel very extended and connected with each other and everything around us, in a very calm peace. Where the love flows with giving and receiving, this is exactly where the heart of meditation lies.

Conclusion

Thank you once again for purchasing this book and I hope you had a good read and that it helped your understanding of meditation.

With the efforts put into writing this book, I hope to have, at least, influenced you to a small extent in trying out the meditation practices that are outlined within the book. Some of these will be less practical for you to try than others and you will decide which way to go when choosing a system of meditation that works for you.

In chapter 1, we looked at the various questions in regard to meditation and answered each of these to give you a fair idea of what the concept is all about. These were common questions asked by people who want to know more about meditation but are borderline about whether this is going to be suited to them. The questions are answered in a clear and straightforward manner, to give you the most information possible. This, in turn, can help you on your journey into deciding whether to incorporate meditation into your lifestyle. You will be very glad you did, if you decide to take up meditation since there are clearly so many benefits to regular practice.

In chapter 2 we focused on what meditation can do for your body and gave an overall general perspective of what to expect from your meditation experience. We introduce the concepts that we will touch on in the book including the basic concepts of meditation. Essentially, we introduce the benefits of meditation and why this book should land number one on your list!

Chapter 3 focused on the various benefits of meditation and how it can help bring about a change in both your mental and physical well being. In this chapter, you found detailed information on why meditation may be the right choice and what it can do to help you from mental health perspective. We described both the mental and health benefits of meditation so that you can see their relevance to your life and also see that you may actually find yourself feeling younger with regular practice of meditation.

In chapter 4, we saw how there are at least 10 different types of meditation practices that you can make use of to beat your stress and lead a happy life. These were described in detail, giving you the basic method used for each and also a detailed description of what each type of meditation helps you with.

In chapter 5, we looked at the mandatory precautions that you must undertake when you decide to take up meditation and also had a brief look at the various conditions in which you must perform it. This chapter also dealt with stumbling blocks that you may encounter during your first attempts at meditation. These are well known and should never put you off the experience because in the early days, it's hard to find that frame of mind that is perfect for meditation though, with practice, you will.

Finally, we saw how you must have reasonable expectations in order to fulfill each and not feel disappointed. Meditation is a therapy and a treatment and not a cure so you have to perform it on a daily basis.

I hope the book allows you to take all the necessary steps forward in your life, which will help you to relieve your life of stresses and also help you lead to maximize your enjoyment of life and all that it has to offer you, within and outside of your immediate understanding. Meditation opens up that understanding and helps you to see clearly the full picture of what life has to offer you.

Good Luck and Namaste.

Acknowlededements

http://www.psychologytoday.com/blog/meditation-modern-life/201208/more-doctors-are-prescribing-meditation

http://www.scientificamerican.com/article/is-meditation-overrated/

http://circoutcomes.ahajournals.org/content/5/6/750.abstract

Bonus Video: Healing Spirit- Guided Meditation for Relaxation, Anxiety, Depression and Self Acceptance

Guided Meditation and Autogenic Training with Healing Voice in Sleeping Music with Delta Waves for Brain Power for Health Care and Relaxation Meditation, against

Anxiety and Depression for a Self Acceptance, ideal After a Long Day Working or Studying, Breathing Exercises and Deep Relaxing New Age Zen Music, Mind, Body & Soul Anti stress Meditation for Chakra Balancing.

Bonus Video: https://www.youtube.com/watch?v=EIJQsE8C5Is

Checkout My Other Books

http://www.amazon.com/Mindfulness-Depression-mindfulness-depression-meditation-ebook/dp/B00X9RRQCG/ref=sr_1_27?s=digital-text&ie=UTF8&qid=1437154345&sr=1-27&keywords=mindfulness

http://www.amazon.com/Yoga-Tranquility--Mindfulness-Meditation-meditation-ebook/dp/B010OEN78I/ref=sr_1_18?s=digital-text&ie=UTF8&qid=1437154384&sr=1-18&keywords=yoga

Made in the USA
Middletown, DE
05 January 2016